GW00647853

HAUNTED KENT TODAY

This still from a video film shot by Martin Emmott shows his wife Janet, and daughter Kirsten, riding at Cobham Manor, but what or who is the Quaker-type figure between them? Story on page 7.

Andrew Green

S.B. Publications

By the same author
Haunted Sussex Today
Mysteries of Surrey
Mysteries of Sussex
Mysteries of London
Our Haunted Kingdom
Ghosts of Tunbridge Wells
Ghosts of the South East
Phantom Ladies
The Ghostly Army
Ghosts of Today
Haunted Houses
Haunted Inns & Taverns
A Caccie de Fantasmi

First published in 1999 by S.B. Publications
c/o 19 Grove Road, Seaford, East Sussex BN25 1TP

© 1999 Andrew Green

ISBN 1 85770 181 X

Typeset by JEM Lewes
Printed in England by Adland Print Group Company Ltd
Unit 11, Bellingham Trading Estate, Franthorne Way, London SE6 3BX
Telephone: 0181 695 6262

Front cover: Michael Jack, professional dowser, shown dowsing with a crystal in March 1998. The white mist is a possible energy source coming from the altar in the ruins of the crypt in Wulfric's Rotunda, Canterbury.

Back cover: see pages 12 and 13

INTRODUCTION

WHENEVER Kent is mentioned, many of those interested in ghosts automatically think of Pluckley as 'the most haunted village in the country' and Blue Bell Hill near Maidstone as the 'home' of the phantom hitch-hiker.

This selection of modern and, I believe genuine hauntings all experienced within living memory – the last 25 years – will perhaps create a new league table as far as village phantoms are concerned, despite the recent entry in the Guinness Book of Records.

One must never forget however, that statistically there are more ghosts of living people than those of the dead. One brilliant example of this is that of Terry Waite being seen in Canterbury Cathedral when he was actually being held hostage in Lebanon.

Kent has suffered invasions, religious battles, smuggling activities, witchcraft, natural disasters and the horrifying effects of international war, especially World War Two, all of which I think, have been instrumental in the traumas and emotional sensations that create apparitions.

But there remain many mysteries, such as that of the Quaker-like figure videod in the Cobham Riding Park, the filmed evidence of incredible poltergeist phenomena in Dover Castle witnessed by a number of scientific investigators including Dr Chris Cherry of Kent University, and the computer in Gravesend inexplicably affected by weird shapes and symbols.

Despite such factual evidence, for some, the unequivocal proof is yet to be achieved. 'Proof is an idol before which even a mathematician tortures himself' Sir Arthur Eddington stated recently. So don't try and figure them out, just accept that Kent remains the most ghost-affected garden of England – and enjoy the spirit of the chase.

Andrew Green
Mountfield 1998

ACKNOWLEDGEMENTS

MY sincere thanks for the help and assistance provided in compiling this collection are due to the following very kind people:

Amber Baylis, DR Bell, David Bill, Victor Brobyn, Rod Carroll, Pamela Chandler, the Hon Alan Clark and Jane Clark, Andrew Clough, Graham Green, Derek Jones, Roger and Trish Jones, Rita Hargreaves, Alan Harradine, Tracy King, Paul Kitchenham, Carolyn Logan-Taylor, Peter Malkin, John Mitchell, Deirdre Morris, Richard Parker, John Parr for the photos, Roy Philips, Brenda
Powell, Maggie Ray, Ken Scott, David and Shirley Spearing, Frank Stevens, Heather Thorne, Rose Urquhart, Wynn Vallé, Bruce Walker, Russell Whiteside and PH Wood, as well as the librarians at Sevenoaks and East Malling, and Barbara Leigh and Andrew Lister of Sevenoaks Reference Library.

I am also greatly indebted to Griselda Cann of Faversham, Martin Emmott for his much appreciated co-operation in supplying the remarkable video picture taken at the Cobham Manor Riding Centre, Margaret Gadd of West Malling, Mark Gardner of *Faversham Times*, Barry Hollis of the *Kent Messenger* Group, Pam Huby of Tunbridge Wells, Michael Jack, Alan Murdie,chairman of the Ghost Club, Ian Peters of Lamberhurst and Lance Railton of the Ghost Club.

Special thanks are also due to Ursula Bull for, despite handicaps, carrying out considerable research in Sevenoaks, Paul Harris for his ever continuing wealth of material covering the Shepway area, Tom Perrott, former chairman of the Ghost Club, for so kindly checking his personal records and supplying a number of marvellous illustrations, Jack Pleasant for his support, photographs and overall assistance and to Sean Tudor of Maidstone for providing so much detail regarding the Blue Bell hauntings. Thanks also to Stephen Benz for his extreme patience and valuable help, but also a very special thanks to Norah Bridget, my wife, for her understanding, advice and considerable patience, and to whom this work is dedicated.

ALLINGTON

Allington Castle

IN 1951 the manor house at Allington, which had been fortified in 1281, was taken over by the Ancient Order of Carmelites, but more recently the nuns moved to Aylesford Priory, and the castle is now privately owned and not open to the public.

During the Tudor period, it was the home of the well known Wyatt family, one of whose members was thought to be the lover of Anne Boleyn. Over the centuries the building declined and was practically derelict when Lord Conway bought it in 1905 to carry out a massive restoration scheme.

The old keep, Solomon's Tower, remains as part of the original building of Sir Stephen de Penchester, and it is here that a ghost of a servant girl has occasionally been witnessed. Another, rather vague claim, implies that she may be seen in the privy garden of the King's Tower.

Celia Botley of Tunbridge Wells told me that during a visit, a few years ago, she learnt that one of the residents was sceptical about the reports until, when sitting downstairs alone one afternoon, he heard the sound of footsteps overhead but could find no cause for the noise, although he felt as if someone were watching him.

The phantom maid is thought to be that of a young woman who was hanged for drowning her illegitimate baby in the moat.

ASHFORD

George Hotel

ONE wonders how many young chambermaids in days gone by were brutally murdered as a result of frustrated passion. Here apparently is such a case, the murderer in this instance being the chef who not only ravished the girl but, on learning of her pregnancy, slit her throat and then hung her body up in the cellar for six weeks, like some animal's carcass. The killer was eventually hanged himself for this horrific murder. It is his unfortunate victim, it is thought, who causes the current spate of phenomena.

Danny Hughes, the manager's son, assured me that the previous owners of the hotel had told him that the ghost of the young girl had definitely been witnessed, not just by them, but by people in the rear bar – the 16th century area of the building – where, coincidentally, a priest's hole was discovered. Additionally there is a series of tunnels, now blocked off, that linked four pubs and the church. There is some evidence too that the hotel was associated with a smuggling gang. In the 18th century, it was also the local excise office for Ashford – an ideal cover for any illegal activities.

The most recent experiences have been of poltergeist activity in which small objects, such as keys, have been thrown around, kettles and lights switched on and off, Mrs Hughes' handbag thrown on the floor and, the most irritating, causing all the hotel guests to complain, the television set being switched on by some unseen force and 'music of a very loud pop variety' is turned up to top volume. This had occurred when the hotel had been closed down for the night and all the staff were in bed.

Danny is unable to offer any explanation as to how such a haunting can be associated with a chambermaid murdered more than 250 years ago.

AYLESFORD

Preston Hall Chest Hospital

IN the past Preston Hall must have been one of the most glorious mansions in Kent,' says Joy Ingle in her excellent little history of the hospital. It certainly boasts of ancient foundations, being associated with the famous Culpepper family. Walter owned it during the reign of King John (1199-1216) and Thomas from 1702 to 1714. The original old manor was demolished in 1848 by Edward Betts, known for his company's construction of the Canadian Pacific Railway, and who built the hospital some two years later.

A local legend relates that an Elizabethan woman would secretly meet her lover 'in a niche at the end of a terrace behind the house', but when a maid encountered the man by mistake, the owner, in a fit of pique or jealousy, murdered him.

The building is currently administered by the Royal British Legion as a medical centre specialising in the treatment and care of chronic chest complaints and non-progessive disabilities.

On a number of occasions cleaning staff have seen the figure of a woman in 'an old style dress' near one of the former bedrooms. An additional 'haunting' has been the disturbing sound of a strong verbal argument between a man and a woman in the same area. Unfortunately the words have been indistinguishable, although sounding 'as if being shouted out by a couple of foreigners'. Elizabethan English would, no doubt, be unintelligible to most of the current population.

BEARSTED

Cobham Manor Riding Centre

IT was here, a few yards from the Pilgrim's Way, in August 1985, that Martin Emmott was videoing his wife Janet and their ten-year-old daughter Kirsten trotting round the circuit on their horses, to create an enjoyable memento of his wife's return to the saddle after some 20 years. Nothing unusual was noted, except that on the following afternoon, when Janet was watching the video, recalling her delights of the ride, she realised that there was something peculiar on the screen. Just behind the figure of her daughter, and in front of the next rider, on a white horse, was 'a ghostly Quaker-like figure'. Martin hurried home immediately on getting a call from his wife, and was so puzzled by what he could see that he took the tape and camera to the local television studios to have it checked by experts. They confirmed that the mysterious figure was 'definite'.

Mrs Emmott, the daughter of a policeman, made a categorical statement that there was absolutely nothing unusual when she was riding on that bridleway.

There are perhaps two incidents that may be related to the mystery. Some

This picture is taken from a video tape made by Martin Emmott of his wife Janet and daughter Kirsten. Who or what is the mystery figure between them?

years previously, a rider attempted to get his horse to jump a gate where Ware Street, Bearsted, joins Weavering Street, but he fell, broke his neck and died. A few months later a neighbour reported that whilst riding in the same area early one morning, he had heard the sounds of a horse breathing and the hooves on the path pass him, but no animal was ever visible. His own horse naturally became very agitated and frightened by the incident, but like the Emmotts, he saw nothing untoward.

James Brummer, owner of the land, had often noted that horses were 'spooked' when approaching that specific pathway, but no explanation was ever found. Could there be any connection with the adjoining Pilgrims' Way?

BIGGIN HILL

Battle of Britain Airfield

WHY is it that so many of the former Battle of Britain airfields are haunted only by ghostly Spitfires, and the sound of their distinctive Merlin engines, for surely other aircraft used the sites? What must be one of the most famous fighter stations during the Second World War is that of Biggin Hill, an airfield that is still affected by the noise of a phantom aircraft hurtling in to land and, seconds later, the sound of a shattering explosion to be followed by 'deathly silence'.

Countless reports have filtered down through the years of these ghostly incidents, the Spitfire being the most reported. This does not answer the question of the involvement of other aircraft, but it should not be forgotten that it was this airfield that became the birthplace of radar. The RDF scheme – radio direction finder – was developed and installed, initially, at Biggin Hill, offering an additional target for German bombers, and accounting for the many dogfights in the area.

Unexplained also is that the haunting seems to occur mainly in January and is combined with the sound of men's voices 'in a party mood'. Sometimes witnesses report seeing a group of three or four misty shapes strolling over what used to be the runway, or moving towards the site of one of the Nissen huts used as a rest centre by the flying crew.

But as the years pass the detail of the figures fades and what used to be seen clearly as the outline of pilots in their flying gear, now appear as 'woolly shapes in bulky uniforms'. Yet they are still haunting. The last report was in January 1997.

BOUGHTON ALUPH

Eastwell Manor

DEVELOPED from an original farmstead belonging to the Aluph family, this small village with its central green, cricket pitch and pavilion, also contains the haunted Eastwell Manor. The original building of 1086 was replaced early in the 20th century. Materials from the old building were used and the Tudor styling attempted to retain some of the earlier atmosphere.

The Manor, standing in sixty two acres of grounds, is a flamboyant reminder of an earlier owner, Sir John de Fonblanque Pennefather who, in the 1920s, employed amongst his substantial staff, an enthusiastic coachman well known for his womanising. It was this that caused the man's downfall and, it is believed, the haunting that affects the house in which he lived. He was found to be trifling with the affections of the wife of a highly respected guest, and was finally caught *in flagrante* and was immediately killed by the cuckolded husband.

In November 1997 I spoke to the senior porter, Alan Standing, who although he had seen nothing untoward, had most certainly experienced some form of haunting in what is now a popular hotel. One evening, only a couple of weeks earlier, he had been playing snooker with a colleague, Ben Prout, when they suddenly heard what sounded like a door slamming, but not actually shutting, for the noise 'clunk, clunk', continued for a few seconds. Both men spent some time trying to find an explanation for the mystifying noise and were beginning to feel a bit on edge because the sound was moving around, sometimes from one of the hollow walls, then from under their feet. Eventually it stopped and they returned to their game, but at about six in the morning Ben jumped up and ran from the room complaining that he had been shocked, 'like feeling electrified'. The sensation came up through the floor, and Ben found his fingers and legs were tingling, and he was unable to continue playing.

An earlier experience of two senior staff members was when, in 1994, they walked into the bar one evening and glanced in the mirror to see the figure of a woman in a white gown standing in the doorway. But on turning to greet what they thought was a guest, they found the room empty.

Another incident was when a honeymoon couple were staying in what had been the coachman's room. Suddenly they rushed out, demanding another room, because all the lights, and the radio, were being switched on and off, and there was a sound of thumping on the floor, like someone kicking it, the couple said.

BRANDS HATCH

Brandshatch Place, Fawkham

JUST off Scratchers Lane, north of the famous racing circuit, visitors can enjoy the facilities of Fredericks, a popular country club incorporated into the Brandshatch Place Hotel, which is said to be 'really haunted'.

When, in Edwardian times, the mansion was the private home of a middle-aged wealthy bachelor, an attractive member of the resident female staff, Mollie, who acted as a housekeeper, fell victim to the owner's advances but was found later to be rather an embarrassment and she suddenly and mysteriously disappeared.

An apparition of a young woman wearing a straight skirted gown with a neatly ironed apron, and carrying a basket of flowers, has been seen gliding through the reception hall, into the kitchen and continuing on into the garden where she vanishes. Witnesses, who include members of the staff and a number of guests, are intrigued by the appearance of what is assumed to be the ghost of the former housekeeper, but a number of questions arise, and only time may provide the answers.

Why does the phantom vanish at a certain spot in the garden, is it perhaps of some significance? What is so symbolic about the basket of flowers? And, of course, if she is not Mollie, who is she and what reason has she for haunting?

The mysterious image was last seen by a member of the hotel's staff in October 1997.

One cheerful aspect is that the young woman causes no fear and her appearances are fully accepted as 'just another visitation'.

BRASTED

Brasted Place

IN the 1960s Brasted Place was established as a college, but it was originally constructed in the 17th century as part of the estate of Walter de Stocket. It formed a portion of his knight's fee during the reign of Edward I. Eventually the manor was purchased, in the 1700s, by John Turton from Sir Robert Heath, and later it became a theological college. According to the Reverend Peter Mullen, there were several reports, during a period of transition prior to the establishing of its theological status in the 1980s, that the resident ghost was 'so solid it was often mistaken for the college chaplain'.

The tall figure wearing a dark grey cassock would stride, albeit silently, through the corridors, and on one occasion was witnessed by Peter Mullen himself.

There have been only a few sightings within the last 25 years though, and the figure has faded in definition somewhat, yet still seems to be on a very purposeful journey.

BRENCHLEY

All Saints' churchyard

John Ferrall, the vicar here in 1581, accused Margaret Simons of witchcraft, of having placed a curse on 'his sonne' because he had pursued her little dog with a knife. She rebuked him to such an extent that within 'five or six daies (he) fell sicke'. Thanks to the ministrations from other witches in the village he recovered, but this report surely establishes that the village was a thriving community during the Civil War period.

A visitor to the village in August, 1988, decided to have a look at the cemetery of the 13th century All Saints Church, and whilst examining some of the old tombstones, became conscious of something. 'Looking up I saw just the head and shoulders of what I took to be a Roman soldier,' he explained. 'He had a close fitting helmet on and was gazing intently in front of him. He looked young and fair of face. As I went towards him and the stone he was studying, he disappeared.'

The inscription on the stone was illegible and, despite investigating the village and the church, Robin Laurence, my informant, was unable to find any mention of a Roman association. Like some others, though, he is of the opinion that the figure could well be that of a Roundhead.

BRIDGE

Bridge Place Country Club

When I interviewed the owner of this popular club in 1973 for one of my earlier books, *Our Haunted Kingdom*, I could not have forseen that some 25 years later I was to learn that the haunting of the manor house, which had been built in 1638 but partly destroyed during the Civil War, was still being experienced. Peter Malkin had originally told me that shortly after he bought the building in 1967, he was astounded to see the figure of a chambermaid, carrying a basket, walk silently through his bedroom. It was, he assured

Peter Malkin, owner of Bridge Place Country Club, at the fireplace where a child's cries are heard.

me, as have other witnesses, most peculiar. More disturbing however, have been the pitiful cries of a small child seemingly coming from a chimney breast in a ground floor room.

When I asked him in June 1998 if anything had occurred since last we spoke, Mr Malkin told me that only two weeks previously, two Dutch guests had heard the sound of the crying and had also seen the vague figure of a woman glide through the room. She wore an old-fashioned bonnet and gown, with an apron, and carried the basket.

In about 1780, the then owner of the house, a man named Taylor, had seduced one of the maids whilst his wife was in Scotland recovering from a long and serious illness. Legend has it that the young woman gave birth to a child and the seducer murdered them both because of the forthcoming return of his wife. 'Perhaps the baby was thrown on to the fire and what we hear now are its cries, over two hundred years later,' Mr Malkin surmises. 'But the appearance of the woman and the basket is intriguing. Maybe she was the midwife.'

Higham Park

DOES the experience of one witness formulate a genuine haunting? Maybe the incident was the start of regular visitations, or even the finalisation of a series. Can one accept that only one person has seen a factual example of phenomena at a particular location at a specific time, more especially as they don't believe in ghosts? There are often such cases that fall into such imponderable categories but this, at Higham, may be seen as the continuation of a haunting perhaps previously un-noticed or simply un-recorded.

Patricia Gibb, one of the owners of this magnificent 14th century country estate, assured me that what she saw, and was able to photograph, initially annoyed and then puzzled her, more especially as she doesn't believe in

On the left is picture 14 on the roll of negatives; on the right, picture 15, taken just seconds later. Pictures: Patricia Gibb.

ghosts. With her colleague, Amanda Harris-Deans, she was busy in the main ballroom restoring one of the beautiful pieces of furniture, when she glanced out to see a man running across a field that only a few days earlier had been carefully seeded to provide a lawn. Grabbing a camera, and shouting 'Get off', she hurriedly took a couple of photographs with the vague idea of being able to show the police later, to identify the intruder. However the figure had vanished well before reaching the gateway, although the period between taking the two pictures could not have been more than three seconds. When the resultant prints were received, the first clearly shows a weird glowing shape surrounding 'a two legged something' captured on the film, but the other, just an empty field.

There have been numerous tales over the years that Count Louis Zborowski, creator of the famous Chitty Chitty Bang Bang car haunts the building that was once his home. The count was killed in 1924. 'Maybe he has returned to look for one of the machines that is supposed to be buried somewhere in the grounds,' Patricia suggested when I spoke to her in July 1998. 'I still cannot believe in ghosts, but no-one can explain to me how a figure of a man can just disappear like that in front of a couple of witnesses.'

13

In the early days of the National Health Service the building was known as Highland Court and between 1952 and 1988 was one of the hospitals in the Canterbury region.

At three o' clock one morning in the late 1970s, Joan Bell, a nurse on night duty, and 'a total unbeliever in ghosts', suddenly noticed the figure of a man standing in a corner of the ward, but because of the placing of one of the beds, he was visible only from the waist up. He glanced at Joan, smiled and vanished.

On discussing the incident with her colleagues, Joan learnt that the apparition had been seen on a number of occasions and his description – wearing a hacking jacket, and having wavy red hair parted centrally, matched that of Zobrowski's chief design engineer, Perry Thomas, who was killed in a crash on the Pendine Sands in 1923.

In the autumn of 1998, a sale of antiques was held in the grounds, and one of the guards supplied by Philips, the auctioneers, having locked up, was walking home past the rear of the building. She glanced back at the house and was puzzled to see a woman carrying a candle moving through one of the rooms on the top floor. Patricia Gibb explained that all the rooms on that floor were locked and empty.

BROOKLAND

THE mysteriously romantic atmosphere of Romney Marsh, especially in the autumn, with the mists rising from streams, drainage gulleys and marshland, together with the remembrance of Dr Syn and his smuggling cohorts, can provide the catalyst for tales of horror and the frightening appearances of weird shapes and indistinguishable figures.

Factually, and perhaps disappointingly, there are few real instances of hauntings. There are a couple of smuggler-created tales of headless horses and riders of course, but occasionally one learns of an incident that can be recorded as genuine and one such experience is, according to Paul Harris, that which Roy Vidler suffered recently.

He was driving home to New Romney, but was still close to the village of Brookland, when out of the swirling mists, a man stepped into the road in front of him and beckoned him to stop. Roy braked as quickly and as hard as possible, but the car passed straight through the figure, before screeching to a halt. The driver, shocked and shaken, went to find the weird apparition, for the shape he had seen was 'wearing a black pointed beard and Elizabethan style clothing', and was 'hardly credible'.

Knowing too of the popularity of the area with film and television producers,

Roy wondered if the character had been involved in some forthcoming production, but after spending several minutes looking for the victim, realised that there was nothing to be seen or found.

He remained a little shaky for some time, especially as he had been completely unable to explain the appearance, and disappearance, of a victim of what seemed to have been a very unpleasant car accident.

CANTERBURY

The Cathedral

ONE of the earliest British tribes to greet Caesar when he landed on the Kentish coast in 55BC, were the Canti, who occupied an area on which Canterbury, Cant-wara-byrig, now stands. The county, the first of the English kingdoms, is one of the few to preserve its earliest British name, according to the historian WS Shears.

The first Christian cathedral was completed here in 597 and used by St Augustine to baptise King Ethelbert of Kent. Like so many ancient buildings, it gained a blood-stained history of murder, fire and general disaster culminating during the Second World War when bombs fell in its grounds.

However the ghosts that frequent the grand edifice are ancient, one thought to be Archbishop Simon Sudbury, who was killed in 1381. Only his torso is believed to be buried within the walls of the cathedral because, for some reason unknown, his head lies in a churchyard in his home county of Suffolk. The 'old phantom', as this ghost was known, has not been seen for some 30 years and, as is common with so many apparitions, its identity remains a mystery. Those who saw it described 'a dignified character with a grey beard and a fair complexion'. Also unidentified, and even more mysterious, is the figure of a monk seen a few years ago by novelist Rhona Martin who, as a result of her experience, became fascinated with the paranormal. The hooded figure used to be seen in the evening by the occasional visitor in the cloisters.

The sound of unaccompanied chanting used to be heard at dusk near the ruins of the old infirmary as well, but no recent incidents have been recorded.

An incredible report made by a woman in Manchester to Graham McEwan, author of *Haunted Churches*, details a brilliant case of a crisis apparition of the living being observed in September 1987. The clearly recognisable figure of Terry Waite, envoy of the Archbishop of Canterbury, was seen standing in front of the tomb of St Augustine, when he was factually being held as a hostage in the Lebanon. The phantasm remained only for a few seconds before gradually fading.

Canterbury Cathedral.

Church of St Margaret

THERE are a number of organised ghost tours in the county, some commercialised with spectral appearances available to order, whilst others, the genuine historical and rational variety, such as that provided by Janet Feaber of the Canterbury Tales attraction, offering factual information for those really interested in the subject. During a recent discussion with Carolyn, I learnt that there seems to be a dearth of modern phenomenal incidents in the city, except perhaps for two. One of these being in the cathedral cloisters and the other, less visual, being experienced at the entrance of St Margaret's Church. Here, a very strong concentration of what may be psychic energy, has notably affected a few visitors, usually the more sensitive. One or two have been so badly influenced by 'the force', that they have been 'near to

Church of St Margaret

fainting', but quickly recover. Some believe that the doorway is the site of some appalling tragedy or terrible incident, the trauma from which has become implanted in the surrounding ancient stonework.

Two other potentially haunted areas within the presentation stage of The Canterbury Tales, are the Tabard Inn scene, where in 1997 a woman visitor felt that something horrible happened on the same spot where other visitors have been 'overwhelmed with emotion', and the Pardoner's Tale, where one psychic felt such a strong presence that she refused to complete her visit.

CHARTHAM DOWN

St Augustine's Hospital

HELEN Crowley was a senior nursing sister at the hospital some years ago, and was responsible for some 60 patients. The ward had locked doors at each end. There was a small, low wattage light to illuminate the

17

whole ward at night, as well as the usual shaded table lamp for the supervisory nurse. Helen said: 'I was writing to my mother one night, and glanced at my watch to realise that being one o'clock, it was time to carry out my rounds. As I got up to get the key to clock in at the other end of the ward, I saw a woman coming towards me, but I seemed to be paralysed and just couldn't move. I could only watch as the mysterious stranger glided nearer. She appeared to be grey all over, dress, hair, face, even her hands which were clasped in front of her, and although she didn't look directly at me, I could sense that her eyes were full of utter sadness.' The figure reached the first bed and bent down, fumbling with the buttons of her dress, getting ready to put on a night gown, but Helen, realising that the bed was already occupied, managed to break the spell and moved rapidly to stop the woman. As she rose to hurry forward, the phantom patient slowly faded away.

Helen was so mystified that she made enquiries from other senior staff members, and learnt that the patient had been seen by others and recognised as one who had committed suicide only a few days earlier. She had originally been admitted following an attempted suicide, was allowed out to do some shopping with her husband, but was never seen alive again. Her body was discovered by two nurses in the linen cupboard at the end of the ward the following morning.

During her shopping spree, the patient had been able to buy some powerful drugs and once back within the hospital, had taken a massive overdose and curled up in the cupboard to die.

CHATHAM

The Theatre Royal

THE Theatre Royal, today a semi-derelict wreck of a building with peeling walls and temporary plastic sheeting for a roof, was built in 1899 and was once the premier theatre in the Medway region. It closed some forty years ago. In its heyday the theatre could accommodate more than 3,000 people. Current plans are to re-open in 1999 or 2000, but the situation is somewhat bleak, for even the stage house now no longer exists, being integrated into the adjoining department store which itself is threatened with demolition and replacement by a new library.

Richard Parker, a former chairman of The Friends of The Theatre Royal, is one of the few to experience a haunting in the theatre, but only of the smell of 'sweet tobacco smoke'. This was confirmed by some members of visiting groups, who have also reported the same phenomena. One woman noticed the 'invisible pipe smoker' in the auditorium where, of course, no smoking is allowed, or had even been experienced since the 1960s. She told Richard that as she walked through a passageway she felt a tap on her shoulder and 'a sudden breath of warm air blown on to the back of her neck'. She turned to see a woman in Victorian clothing and thought she heard a voice asking 'Where's the major?'

A certain amount of poltergeist activity was experienced by a group of policemen who went into the room where the disturbances had been reported. They noted the chaos of upturned chairs and tables, heard a couple of doors slamming and weird footsteps, decided to leave in rather a hurry and refused to return. Another investigation team replaced them, but when they too heard the same mysterious and unaccountable banging, they agreed to leave the building to the ghosts.

Stories to account for the haunting include that of an acrobat who became so depressed after making a number of serious mistakes during one performance that he hanged himself from the gallery the next day. No apparitions have actually been witnessed, or felt, for some thirty-five years, and the idea that the old building still houses six phantoms, is beginning, presumably like the ghosts themselves, to fade.

CHILHAM

Chilham Castle

THE keep of the old Norman castle at Chilham is today used for mediaeval banquets and similar popular functions, some of which are associated with demonstrations of hawking and hunting by the resident keeper of several impressive birds of prey. I visited the keep in 1975 and learnt that only a couple of years earlier a young woman acting as a serving wench at one of the weekend parties, when outside waiting to greet the guests, saw the figure of an older woman approaching the wall that abuts the keep, and appear to melt into it. Shortly after

Chilham Castle

19

wards, two members of another party commented on the magnificent gown of the woman standing by the old wall and were astounded to learn later that she was an unknown ghost. From the roof directly over the ladies powder room, weird and mysterious sounds have often been heard, like those of someone dragging heavy pieces of furniture about, it is said, but the only equipment on the roof that I could find, were a prominent weather vane and a large and immovable water cistern.

Like my companion and the rather nervous guide with us, I had heard the mysterious noises that still remain unexplained. They certainly cannot be those of the movement of the weather vane. The only other incident was the sudden drop in temperature when nearing the instrument. We were told that during the Norman period several hundred prisoners were kept in the lower section of the tower in what must have been appalling conditions, but the female figure is of a much later period and neither seem to be connected with the weird scratchings on the roof, anyway.

DENTON

Tappington Hall Farm

NESTLING in a small valley of the rural countryside near the Canterbury road and Snode Hill, Tappington Hall is a large privately owned farmhouse featured by the Reverend Barham in his famous *Ingoldsby Legends*. The 700-year-old hall house has Elizabethan and later additions.

The hall is haunted, it is said, although the current owner, Andrew Clough, has never himself seen any phenomena.

During the latter half of 1997 twelve investigators from a local psychical research society held an all-night vigil in the building. They found that their camera equipment failed to work properly in one of the bedrooms and also in the area of the stairway. The sound of faint footsteps, for which no explanation could be offered, were recorded as well.

The main story about the haunting of the hall is of two brothers, a Roundhead and a Cavalier, who had a fight on the stairs with the result that one was killed, and it is his ghost that roams the house. However there are reports of guests witnessing a grey lady seen looking out of the south facing bedroom window, and a friend of the owner told him of seeing an unpleasant face suddenly appearing and gazing at him, when he was in bed. The owner's daughter Laura also experienced the feeling of being watched and hearing the inexplicable footsteps.

In 1980 the local *Evening Post* published a feature on the hall telling the

Tappington Hall Farm

story of three murderers who called upon a witch to help them with a crime. She agreed to assist by providing a special charm made from a hand severed from a corpse hanging in a nearby gibbet, together with five locks of hair from its head. Believing that they were safe, the trio quickly travelled to Tappington Hall where they killed the owner and moved to the Crown Hotel in Rochester to celebrate their success in stealing many golden ornaments and jewels. But a servant who witnessed the crime was able to convince the local law officers of the horror, and the three killers were caught and hanged, whilst the associate, the witch, with the grisly hand hanging from her neck, was thrown into a nearby pond. Whether this tale can be connected with the current phenomena is doubtful; perhaps one day further details will be available.

DOVER

Dover Castle

DOVER Castle, which dates from the 12th century, houses two chapels, the former secret underground command centre which played such a vital role in the Second World War, and the mediaeval underground works which were adapted to protect England from Napoleon's projected attack. It also contains a number of locations haunted by 'sights and sounds belonging to earlier days', together with inexplicable and weird physical phenomena.

An investigation into the hauntings was organised in 1991 by Robin

Dover Castle

Laurence and the Thanet Research Unit. A Meridian Television team, including Mike Debden, the presenter, sixteen members of the research group, Dr Chris Cherry of Kent University, representatives of the Association for the Scientific Study of Anamolous Phenomena, John Spencer, a fellow author and researcher and Dr Peter Moore, carried out an all night vigil, with some incredible results.

No less than eight specific locations were covered by the team members in a well organised rota system, both in the keep and the underground works. In the former, witnesses – staff as well as visitors – had often reported seeing a male figure in 17th century clothing of a cavalier style, later identified as being of the 1610-1630 period, and a woman wearing a red flowing dress.

The underground works area has produced reports of a 17th century pikeman, seen in 1979, as well as a man in a blue cloak, which some feel could well be the same individual as that sighted in the keep. In the summer of 1991 an American visitor with his wife commented on the realistic screams and moans that they heard near St John's Tower, thinking, erroneously, that an audio tape of sound effects was being played. It is this tower where most of the inexplicable incidents occur, the sound of banging doors, 'a really heavy wooden door being slammed shut', being the most common description.

What the investigators did not realise was that this was to be dramatically recorded not only on their tape recorders, but also on their video camera, later

22

to be shown on a Meridian mini-documentary programme. To see a pair of massive doors being shaken at 5.20 in the morning, as if by some huge invisible giant, for some seconds, was to many viewers, let alone the investigators, an incredible and undeniable example of proof of poltergeist phenomena. During the vigil a shadowy figure was also seen by two members of the research team, moving up the stairway, but unfortunately it was never identified.

Dover Castle is clearly haunted by a variety of phenomena experienced by members of the staff, visitors and tourists alike. Adding to the catalogue are ghostly smells. In 1996 one of the custodians stated that there are three different types of odour; one was that of an unwashed man which was so strong that she turned to see who was responsible, but there was no-one to be seen; another, more acceptable smell is that of horse manure, despite the fact that horses have never been kept in the keep. The third is so vague that it defies recognition or identification, and is described as 'some sort of old style perfume'.

The phenomena continues, for in November 1997 it was confirmed that the inexplicable bangings and some of the footsteps are still to be heard, but more noteworthy are the sounds of two men talking in the Dynamo Room. Many visitors arriving in the underground power centre also hear what they believe to be the ghostly voices of Winston Churchill discussing the Dunkirk evacuation with Admiral Ramsey, even though no tape recording of such a conversation is available, let alone played.

More recently some members of the research project clearly heard the sounds of a woman sobbing and the custodians admit that they had seen the figure of a woman in 'a darkish crinoline' in the same locality.

EAST MALLING

Bradbourne House

CURRENTLY this 400-year-old manor house is home to the East Malling Research Station and Bradbourne House Trust under the directorship of Dr Jim Quinlan who, with Margaret Gadd, has provided details of the building's ghostly manifestations.

Within the last ten years the striking figure of a tall and distinguished looking man has been witnessed near the main gateway of the house. Initially he was believed to be the ghost of the former owner, Sir Thomas Twisden, first baronet of Bradbourne, whose portrait hangs in the Judges Room.

Judge Twisden fell foul of Thomas Cromwell in 1655, and was arrested, but he was eventually released from the Tower after only a few weeks' imprisonment on charges of 'sedition and subversion of the present Government'. Thomas had bought the ancient moated house from George Catlyn.

Locals believe that another member of the family, Sir Roger Twisden, the fifth baronet, also haunts the area. His ghost has been seen on a quarter mile section of the New Road leading to the church. This distinctive figure was last sighted by a couple of early morning workmen in 1968. Having been told of the local custom, they called out 'Good morning Sir Roger', only to see the phantom vanish in front of them.

Nevertheless the figure described by witnesses is dressed in Victorian style clothing, certainly not that of the 17th century, and he was seen in the vicinity of the church gate, not that of his former home.

Hoath Wood

ONE evening in 1984 a regional postmaster who had been driving north along Red Hill turned left into Teston Road and suddenly saw 'the peculiar figure of what looked like half a man come out of the woods'. He slowed down to see the figure a little closer, and then realised that he could see nothing above his shoulders. 'The huge collar of what seemed like some form of cloak hid nothing but a blank space.' The witness, by now a little apprehensive, braked and was about to get out of his car, when the figure just faded away.

It was only later that the postman learnt that the ghosts of a murderous, 18th century highwayman, his accomplice, and of his poor victim, were often reported in the area.

EASTWELL

Eastwell Park Lake

AT the south western end of Eastwell Park, north of Ashford and off the Faversham Road, a huge lake borders Aviary Wood and the remains of St Mary's Church, associated with the tomb of Richard Plantagenet, who died in December 1550. The Bethersden marble tomb has been vandalised several times, but was now, thanks to my colleague Michael Jack of Hythe, a fellow author and researcher, it is being well maintained.

The real identity of Richard is a mystery although one report states that he was the son of Richard III – but because of the success in the Wars of the Roses by the Earl of Richmond, he was forced to remain 'a mere labourer' under the care of Sir Thomas Mayle, who built the great house in the park.

Any connection with this and the haunting here, is doubtful, but it is only a few yards from the tomb, and the adjoining lake on the other side of the road leading to Home Farm, that several ramblers have been affected by the weird atmosphere. 'It is rather a creepy place,' said a local resident, 'and I care not to linger when the light is fad-

The devastated tomb of Richard Plantagenet, since repaired by Michael Jack

ing'. One of the most recent incidents was that experienced by a member of the staff employed by Charles Bates, who bought Lake House and the Eastwell estate a few years ago, but then sold it and moved away. Her brother-in-law's dog was being walked by the church gates but suddenly, for no apparent reason, stopped and refused to go any nearer the building, finally turning and fleeing through the shrubland. The dog's owner stood by the gate and noticed a strange figure moving around the churchyard.

In the late 1970s there was a small rotting jetty protruding out into the lake, once used by the long forgotten warden as a 'port' for his small rowing boat. In April 1975 a couple from Folkestone, on a ramble, were pushing through the overgrown brambles and on reaching a point a few yards from the jetty, suddenly stopped. 'We heard footsteps coming towards us, we could see the shrubs and bushes being thrust aside and heard a loud rustling as the walker approached, but there was no-one and nothing there,' I was told.

Years earlier the fourteen-year-old son of a gamekeeper had taken the boat on to the lake, against his parents' wishes, and accidentally overturned the craft as it reached the jetty. His semi-conscious body was dragged on to the platform by one of his friends, but the lad died before reaching medical help.

ELMSTEAD

Elchin Hill

IN any ancient area one can expect, perhaps, to find some rather unusual place names, but here there seems to be quite a unique collection. Hill

Street Bottom joins Whatsole Street at Little Pett opposite Elchin Hill from the junction with School Hill and Glory Lane. The well known Roman Stone Street lies a mere half mile to the east past Spong Wood, and on the opposite side, Mockbeggar. But it's Elchin Hill with its notorious dog leg bend that is the point of ghostly interest.

Originally called Hell Chine Hill, it must have been, and in fact still is, a real danger spot for any unwary traveller. Over the past few years a car smashed through a gate at the bottom of the hill although there was nothing wrong with the brakes, or the driver. A Volvo and a horse box broke down at the same spot for no reason; motorcycles and pedal cycles have also been affected and some five years ago a member of a cycling club died of a heart attack when reaching the vicious bend at the crest of the hill.

About 25 years ago a young woman shot herself in the same locality, and some ten years ago local man Albert Denny was out shooting rabbits one Sunday morning when he glanced towards the road to see an old coach drawn by two horses with the driver hunched over the box, coming down the hill towards him. He broke his gun and moved across the field to see more of the unusual vehicle, but it had vanished.

It was later thought to be the phantom of the Honeywoods coach that had got out of control many years before. As it rushed around the corner, the central shaft speared a nearby oak tree and one of the horses was killed.

In 1982 Jenny Denny, Mr Denny's cousin, was out riding on a 'glorious sun-shiny day' when she suddenly noticed some unusual figures about a quarter of a mile away. 'It was a large dark horse with a rider wearing a huge hat, like a tricorn, three cornered,' she said. 'My mount watched the couple approach down the hill, but then suddenly, there was nothing there. There was certainly nothing to frighten us although my horse did seem a little nervous for a few minutes after that.'

FAVERSHAM

Arden's House

IN 1551 Alice Arden and her lover murdered Thomas, her husband, who was the mayor of Faversham at the time. The crime attracted so much attention that eventually a play was written, allegedly by Shakespeare, which is still performed in the garden of the murder site.

There are records of some very unsavoury details of the killing, including bloodstains that refuse to be cleaned, but the ghost that has been seen by a

26

nephew of Roy and Norma Pleasance, the owners of the affected property, was that of a monk, standing in a space adjoining the bottom of a priest's hole in the bathroom. Roy has often heard mysterious footsteps in the top floor stone built attic, which was once used as a chapel. Some friends and even members of the family freely admit to being a little uneasy when in the area, although the rooms are large and far from gloomy. 'It's just a peculiar atmosphere in there,' said one guest. 'It's not evil, but just uncomfortable.'

Originally the house was part of the massive Faversham Abbey which was constructed in 1147.

Fleur de Lis and Good Witch Cafe

THIS ancient and fascinating building, housing a bookshop and, in the cellars, an intriguing museum, was once a pub with stabling for horses. Allegedly, a flagstone in the yard conceals the entrance to a tunnel connected to an nearby inn which was at one time used by a gang of local smugglers. Wendy Williams, manager of the centre, told me that although she had experienced no visible phenomena, she had heard the telephone exchange exhibit ringing at nine in the morning. This equipment – a Unit Automatic Exchange – the size of a large wardrobe, dates from the 1950s and came originally from Littlebourne, near Canterbury. According to the experts, it is impossible for Wendy to have heard what she did. The exchange is not connected to any electrical power. What has been witnessed in the museum by a previous manager, and was seen again in 1996, was the figure of a woman in a white frock coat who came from behind the telephonic display and disappeared into the wall behind the stairs. It is known that this is the spot where there used to be a door leading to a long passageway. For some reason unexplained, it was thought she was the wife of an ostler.

Another wraith reported recently by two independent visitors was that of a man in an orange jerkin sitting on a barrel in the corner of the cellar.

There is some belief that these two figures may be, in some way, associated with the murder of the mayor Thomas Arden in the 19th century, for it was in the Fleur de Lis pub that the plans for his killing were formulated.

In October 1996 the *Faversham Times* reported that Harold Daretsky, one of the owners of the adjoining Good Witch Cafe, had been puzzled by the sudden failing of a new toaster which inexplicably started to operate a few seconds later. It stopped again and refused to work until a replacement was purchased, when it 'sprung into life as soon as the substitute was connected'. The weirdest incident however, was when Harold felt something unseen walk past him, three times, which was connected, he believes, with the sound of laughter coming from the empty upper floor and which had been heard by a customer of the next door bookshop, Stonebridge Books. It is this shop that has also experienced some poltergeist activity in which lights and the radio have suddenly come on by themselves and, on one occasion, a paperback book flew straight across the room.

Guildhall

DURING a council committee meeting in the Guildhall one evening in November, 1997, members' discussions were suddenly interupted by the sound of heavy footsteps on the stairs, and then in the Council Chamber itself. Bill Reeves, one of the councillors, went immediately to investigate and closed the outer door to ensure that no-one could enter without a key.

Trying to forget the incident, the group re-assembled, but within only a few minutes the sound of 'deliberate and heavy pacing' could be heard in the chamber again. Bill Reeves told the *Faversham Times*: 'You could hear the floorboards creaking and I was utterly convinced that there was someone in the next door room.' The search for the invisible visitor was resumed with three colleagues, including Mrs Elliott, a former mayor, who recommended that all the lights in the building be switched on, but the sounds continued, making the atmosphere 'even creepier'. Only when the town sergeant, Ron Smisson, arrived to enquire the reason for the entrance door being shut, did the sounds cease. Andrea Ingham, the town's assistant group co-ordinator, confirmed that she had heard the floorboards creaking and said that it was all 'a bit weird and spooky'.

The Guildhall, Faversham

Faversham Times reporter, Mark Gardner, told me that this was not an isolated case of a haunting in the Guildhall. Arthur Percival a well-known local historian, had heard the sound of a woman's voice on the stairway on two separate occasions when attending a mid-week meeting some weeks earlier, and another witness had reported hearing the mysterious footsteps in the committee room; so far, no explanation has been found to account for them.

The building was used as a court for more than a hundred years and there has been the suggestion that the ghost of some aggrieved complainant or even a former criminal may be responsible.

Gullivers

VICTOR Brobyn, the new tenant, moved into this old building to open a garden equipment shop in 1982 and started to carry out a major refitting and renovation project, which necessitated calling in two shopfitters from Tilbury. The amount of work involved also meant working in the cellars for a couple of days, but Victor was told that both the workmen were so uncomfortable 'because of the weird atmosphere' that one of them refused to continue, and returned to Tilbury, leaving his colleague to request some other work site. Shortly afterwards a carpenter refused to continue working in the same area, explaining that he kept on coming out in cold sweats, which Victor had also experienced, but preferred to ignore, even though the sensation was unaccountable.

To celebrate the fiftieth birthday of one of the assistant managers, a little time later, Victor took a group photograph in the newly decorated cellar, but was more than a little puzzled by the peculiar cloud-like shape that mars a large portion of the picture. The photograph was borrowed by a staff member who has now left, and the whereabouts is unknown.

On making enquiries, he learned that sometime in the 1900s, a man hanged himself there, which Victor feels may explain the uncomfortable feeling that visitors report whenever in that part of the ancient property.

The owner, David Bell of Oare, told me in 1998 of his young daughter's experience, about 25 years earlier, when accompanying him down the very steep spiral staircase, to collect some wood and coal for the fire. 'Kathryn suddenly stopped about three steps from the bottom and stood transfixed, pointing and staring into a dark corner of the cellar, saying "pretty lady".' After a second or so she regained her normal self as if nothing had happened, but confirming that there is certainly something inexplicable in the area, David's alsatian, Jason, flatly refuses to venture anywhere near the stairs.

Associated with what is, to Mr Bell, an invisible phantom of a woman, was the genuine haunting of the last coaching inn in Kent, The Ship Hotel, now lying derelict. Of the same age as Gullivers, both about 1250, the Ship was a highly popular tavern but was also affected by the 'visitations of the ghost of an oldish, but really beautiful lady' right up to the time when the place closed down. Is there perhaps, some connecting tunnel between the two estabishments and a romantic tale to provide a link ? I doubt if we will ever know.

Shipwright's Arms, Hollow Shore

THE owner of this 300 year old pub, Rod Carroll, assured me in 1997 that the 'ghost or whatever', is still active here. 'My son Simon and a number of my old regulars can confirm that', he said.

The explanation for the poltergeist activity, frequent bangings and the weird and inexplicable movement of furniture and fittings such as ashtrays, glasses, bottles and the like, is that the ghost of an old sailor is responsible.

It seems that many years ago, a ship foundered in the Swale, a few yards from Oare, and a survivor managed to crawl to the nearest building, this weatherboarded cottage, as it was at the time, and tapped on the door. The owner, feeling that it might be unwise to open up at that time of night, shouted from an upstairs window for the stranger to go away, and proceeded to lock up. When he opened the pub in the morning he found the drowned body of the sailor, jammed up against the doorway.

Some twenty years ago, a previous owner, Eileen Tester, saw the figure of a thickset man, of medium height, dressed in a reefer-type jacket, a style that

The Shipwrights's Arms

was popular among Victorian seamen, standing in the bedroom one evening. She also witnessed another mystery visitor, sitting in the small room next to the bar, shortly before he, too, vanished.

Mrs Jemmett, a member of the staff at the time, also noticed the phantom customer, but Tony Girling, a worker in the nearby boatyard, actually saw a bearded man wearing a long black coat enter the bar, turn round and vanish. 'He just went,' he said.

A fireback similar to that fished from the sea by the Dutch sea captain

In 1995 the pub gained media interest when the *Sunday Telegraph* reported that the landlord, Simon Claxton, was another who had experienced the haunting, but he believed that the unknown figure was that of a Dutch sea captain, bringing a cast iron religious icon ashore. It was so heavy and the man was so exhausted that he collapsed in the doorway.

The evidence for this was later dredged up and has become a fixture in the pub – an early fire-back.

The visits of the wraith have always been heralded by the strong smell of tobacco and rum, strengthening the idea of it being a sailor or sea captain.

Priory Church, Davington

NEAR to the site of a vanished priory, recalled by the names of nearby Priory Row and Priory Road, lies the priory church, which at one time had two towers, supposed to have inspired the twin towers of Reculver. Two nuns from the village were shipwrecked in nearby Herne Bay, and the one who was saved had the new church built as a memorial to her unfortunate sister who drowned. The remains of the priory are said to be under the playing fields of Faversham's grammar school.

Within the last few years the figure of a nun has been noticed gliding between the pews of the priory church, but it vanishes on reaching a particular spot in the nave.

Reports of the apparition, mainly by volunteers who help to maintain and clean the building, are associated with other claims of a spectral monk being seen at the top of Davington Hill, producing the usual romantic ideas of an illicit love affair, for which there is, at least so far, no evidence.

Court Street Brewery

THERE is a long tradition of brewing in Faversham, even before Shepherd Neame built its premises here in 1698. With such a long history of occupation, it is not unexpected to find evidence of genuine hauntings in existence and so impressive are they that serious research groups, such as from the renowned Ghost Club, founded in 1862, have carried out extensive investigations, the latest being in December 1996. One of the affected sites is the boardroom on the ground floor, which some of the female staff are reluctant to enter because of 'the shadowy figure seen standing in a corner of the room, behind the door'. A recent witness described the figure as 'a small man in a dark suit' who vanished when his identity was queried.

Another specific site is an area in the main brew house, where another staff member saw 'a pair of legs in dark trousers disappearing up the stairs'. In the corridor leading to the chairman's office, Sue Tarris, one of the secretarial staff, heard footsteps pass her office window and saw 'the top half of a man' glide past. She expected the unknown visitor to return, but when he failed to do so, she went to investigate and found the corridor empty. The man was wearing 'a black coat with a round collar' and is thought to be the shade of Eustace Neame who was head clerk in the bottling department in 1906. He was, to quote one of the executives, 'a brilliant cricketer, golfer and snooker player, but sometimes rather lacking in a desire to work'.

The store room is another haunted area, for in August 1996, when the Ghost Club returned, one of the team saw 'a man in his late fifties, crouching down with his hands on his knees'. A colleague was called in to confirm the existence of the stranger, but he could see nothing, although the hairs on the back of his head stood up. In this case however, the apparition is thought to be that of an unfortunate worker who fell into one of the vats of beer many years ago.

Two of the most recent incidents were recorded in the first floor corridor. In one there was the noise of 'laboured breathing' coming from the middle of the metal staircase leading to the reception office. In the second a trail of wet footprints led to a brick wall and appeared to go right through it.

FOLKESTONE

The Bayle

IN 1979 when the weather was 'suitable', Mrs Ludgate would sit in her back garden among the 16th century cottages off Mercery Lane, and enjoy the view of the sea and general outlook over Folkestone. The garden has a 15ft high wall built in a half moon shape around it, and it was at the far end that Mrs Ludgate had 'once or twice', seen a group of 'about twelve men working on the site and occasionally in an open-sided shack where they seemed to be making gardening tools'.

Slightly puzzled by their appearance, she thought that they might be phantoms of poor working mendicants, members of a monastic order subsisting purely on alms provided by charity. The figures were dressed in brown habits, although the adjoining church, one of the first Norman buildings of 1095, accommodated Benedictine monks, who wore black clothing. However, a few feet away a priory existed until its destruction only eight years after it was built in 1538, and it is this community that may well have employed groups of travelling monks to assist in their work. Ruins of this building could still be seen in the 1980s.

Mrs Ludgate was not the sole observer of the ghostly group, for friends and a number of visitors have remarked on the figures that 'seem suddenly to vanish after only a few seconds'.

Clifton Hotel

HERE, a few years ago, in one of the town's premier hotels, a resident killed herself in a fourth floor bedroom. It is believed that the reason was a broken romance.

In a certain room on the floor below a number of guests have, like some of the staff, experienced 'rather loud but completely unaccountable noises, like furniture being moved about'. The room above, from which the sounds emanate, has remained empty for some time.

Early in 1995 a night porter left the hotel rather hurriedly after reporting that on the previous night he was 'grabbed by an invisible hand' as he approached the affected room.

But it is on another floor, the fourth, that a businessman was woken in the early hours, to see the figure of a woman in a 'long white night-gown', standing at the end of the bed. 'All I felt was extreme sadness, great sorrow, utter misery when I looked at her,' said the witness. The apparition began to fade away after about half a minute. The room was where the suicide occurred.

Underhill House

In 1975, with two fellow researchers, Bill Buckman and Dick Godden of Folkestone, I interviewed a number of people, including a Major Bevan, whilst investigating the haunting of a derelict building known then as Lord

33

Underhill House

Beachborough House; at that time it was owned by the military at Shorncliffe Camp. The building, constructed in 1840, was provided as a home for the brigadier in charge of the camp.

Multiple hauntings have been reported in the house, caused, it is said, by four violent deaths.

Shortly before the Second World War a young lieutenant, having got into debt through excessive gambling, decided that the only answer was to shoot himself, after pleading unsuccessfuly with the general for help. This he did, outside the commander's office on the ground floor.

A few years earlier, in 1932, a tragedy was set in motion when the batman of the resident brigadier strangled his girl friend for being unfaithful, but was caught only minutes later. The following morning, realising he would be unable to escape the law, the young man grabbed his officer's revolver, and shot himself – on the landing of the servant's staircase.

The fourth death was yet another suicide. The government of the day had decided to carry out a massive reduction of defence costs, which involved the merging of two of the regiments at Shorncliffe. This resulted in the compulsory retirement of one of the colonel padres who, having served practically a life time in the army, realised that he was totally unable to cope with civvy street. Within days of the announcement his body was found hanging from a water supply pipe in an airing cupboard on the first floor landing.

By the time the army relinquished the building as a semi-private residence the haunting had become well established. A disembodied voice was heard from the

The servants' staircase

34

empty kitchens; one of the former servants saw the figure of 'an old man in a pepper and salt suit bending down in a cupboard examining wine racks', only to vanish when approached; a quantity of cutlery disappeared minutes before a final official function was held in 1973; and what was considered to be 'a really mysterious incident', was the movement of a huge laundry basket from the hallway to the airing cupboard on the first floor, by some unseen force. It was so heavy that it had taken four men to carry it in.

The incident that I found personally mystifying, was when we three were about to leave for a lunch break. We started to go down the stairs, Bill Buckman first, me following and Dick immediately behind me, when we all heard the sudden tinkling of glass in the corridor, and on turning round, Dick and I both saw a lamp bulb, some ten feet away, rocking on the floor. It was warm when I picked it up, yet it could not have been used as the electricity supply had been cut off some months earlier. There was only one empty lamp socket in a bedroom leading off the corridor and I knew that Dick Godden had not thrown it there. The filament was still intact, so what, we wondered, caused the sound? Some months later a suggestion was made that the sound was more like that of a chandelier glass, and of course, when inhabited, there had been such a unit in that main bedroom.

The house was burnt down 'mysteriously' in 1978 through, according to military sources, 'an electrical fault', despite there being no power connected for the previous three years.

In 1993 Adrian and Maria Coombs-Hoar of Dover visited the site with several other serious researchers, and recorded the sighting of 'strange figures amongst the surrounding shrubland' including that of 'a ghostly form of a woman' and a man 'looking rather vacant, wearing an army officer's great coat'. Several multi-coloured lights were also seen in the area during the period of their visits, which remain, like the apparitions, unexplained.

GOUDHURST

Pattyndenne Manor

ONCE the home of the standard bearer to Henry VIII, who also used the building as a hunting lodge, Pattyndenne Manor appears little changed since it was built as an early domestic property in the 15th century. Today it can be seen as a lived-in family home with a warm, friendly and comforting atmosphere, although containing a mysterious prison dating from 1290.

Some twenty five years ago David and Shirley Spearing moved in to what was then 'a rather sombre, cold building', with the aim of transforming it into a showplace of Kentish skills and crafts, open to the public. It was whilst Shirley was putting up curtains that an unknown wraith made its first appearance. 'He was standing beside me,' she said, 'and as I turned away from the window, it was suddenly like looking through a green transparency which faded as I watched, although I was able to make out the shape of a man in old style clothing, certainly no-one from this age, but it was all too quick. I told no-one at the time, because I thought people would say I was mad.'

Some weeks later however, when workmen moved in to complete the restoration programme, Shirley saw the phantom figure a number of times and felt that the disturbance of the surroundings was in some way responsible.

'After a couple of sightings', she told me, 'I was able to recognise that he was wearing pre-Elizabethan clothing, with a short cloak, but could not see his feet and realised that the level of the original landing where he made his entrance, so to speak, was a couple of inches lower down'.

Some reports of the ghost having been seen by members of the work force reached the owners, who were delighted to learn that other people had witnessed him. He is now affectionately called 'Thomas' by the family, who are continuing to try and find out more about their uninvited guest. They have noted, though, that he is more likely to be seen when there is a thunderstorm about and Tess, their youngest daughter confirms that 'he really is a friendly, kind sort of person'.

Another paranormal incident experienced here, perhaps more by casual visitors, is the inexplicable smell of spices in the original banqueting hall. Two recent guests, Rod and Lesley Eldridge, reported the 'delightful perfume of spices, or incense' when they visited the Manor late in 1997. Like Shirley, they felt that they were merely sharing the experience with an often unseen but certainly 'kindly' entity.

GRAVESEND

Heritage House

THIS 18th century, four storey building, practically adjoining The Three Daws (claimed to be the county's oldest pub) comprises an amalgam of business ventures. In August 1996 Tony Tomkins noticed that his computer screen had an altered date setting for no obvious reason, and then, whilst he watched, 'weird shapes and symbols that were not even on the keyboard suddenly appeared,' he said. 'It was a bit hairy.' On discussing the incident with a neighbouring tenant, journalist Anne Pass, he learnt that she too had experienced similar malfunctions of her computer system, together with other phenomena. One Saturday morning, when by herself in the building, Anne heard the sounds of other people moving around in one of the other offices. 'At one time it sounded like a person using an electric typewriter, but there was no-one there. The room was completely empty'.

On another occasion, having moved to a different part of the building and during the process of erecting shelves and fitted cupboards, the workforce of one of the companies realised that despite the intense heat outside, 'the room felt, suddenly, like a walk-in deep freeze, or the coldest fridge imaginable'. Shortly after completing the move, 'objects started to shift around on their own,' one of the team explained. 'A missing cheque was found, fresh and undamaged, under a pile of leaves in the garden leading to the Hole in the Wall Alley, the electric kettle suddenly turned itself on and off and the lights would flicker inexplicably.'

Smells are not unknown with poltergeist activity, but in this case it was the odour, or to some, the perfume of baking bread, that pervaded the landing, accompanied by the mouth watering smell of frying bacon. No explanation could be found for any of these peculiarities. Margaret Goulding, a colleague of Tony Tomkins, said that by leaning against the kitchen wall near to where the smell originates, it is possible to feel heat, as if there is a fire there, but the kitchen itself is cold.

All three witnesses seem to think that the mischievous pranks may, in some way, be associated with the ghost of Pocahontas, the young American Indian girl who came to England in 1616 as the wife of a widower, John Rolfe. Within a year she was so homesick that she travelled to Gravesend to board a boat back to her homeland, but suddenly she was taken ill and died, aged only twenty two.

HAWKINGE

Airfield

A NOTHER Battle of Britain fighter aircraft station, Hawkinge is surrounded by evocatively named sites such as Gibraltar and Gibraltar Lane; it adjoins Western Boundary, the well known ancient Pilgrim's Way to the south, and on the eastern edge is the large Killing Wood. To the north of Aerodrome Road, lies the crematorium and cemetery.

On a number of occasions in the past few years the phantom of a former Spitfire pilot has been witnessed in the area. His normal location seems to be the approaches to the cemetery but in two incidents he was seen coming from the Killing Wood, wearing complete flying gear, jacket, boots and goggles, but he vanished when approached by a couple taking an evening stroll.

One of the most intriguing incidents of recent years occurred in March 1998 when a woman living in one of the new houses built on the aerodrome site rushed into the office of the Kent Battle of Britain Museum, to report that for nearly half a minute water suddenly came rushing down from the roof of her house and stopped as suddenly as it started. No explanation could be found, for there had been no rain and no-one was found using a hosepipe, but researches indicated that the house was on the site of the an engine shed into which a Spitfire had crashed when coming in to land. The connection with water remains baffling, but the hauntings continue.

HEAVERHAM

The Chequers

THIS 17th century pub near Kemsing, in a rural area somewhat divided by the M26, has fairly recently been developed into a fashionable restaurant, but it also retains a weird sort of haunting.

In 1981 waitress Anne Smiley was showing guests to their tables for a special function, when she glanced down to see a pair of legs beside her own, wearing what she described as 'cavalier type thigh boots'. But on looking up she realised that there was no body, and departed to find the manager to see if he could provide an answer. He could not, but reminded her of the figure of a man in 'a cavalier costume' seen in the public bar on more than one occasion.

It is said that during the Civil War two high ranking officers were discussing strategic plans for a campaign, only to realise that a Cavalier standing near them had been listening to their conversation. For safety's sake they decided to 'dispatch the potential danger' and hanged the man in what, centuries later, became the ladies lavatory. It was here that a number of visitors have felt 'decidely uncomfortable' – to such an extent that new lavatories were created during the renovation, and the area is now used solely for storage purposes.

HYTHE

Malthouse Arcade

ONE of the original Cinque Ports, and once sited on a lagoon sheltered by the Dymchurch Wall – a lengthy ridge of pebbles – Hythe is a delightful town of narrow streets and a famous church offering a strange collection of skulls and bones displayed in the adjoining crypt. The wooden based building known as Malthouse Arcade at the western end of the town was built in the 1600s as a bonded warehouse, when Hythe was more closely linked with the sea. It was taken over by Mackesons, the brewers, who used it for many years before moving out, leaving the old building to become derelict.

In 1974 it was restored and became a popular trading centre comprising some thirty stalls selling antiques, books, pictures, pottery and souvenirs of the past. One of the original stall holders was Winifred Vallé, who told me during a visit in November 1997 of an unusual incident she had experienced ten years earlier.

'It was about 8.15 on a Friday morning, when I was alone, preparing the stock for the following day's influx of tourists, when I noticed a man coming up the staircase at the end of the corridor. He was about thirty years old and wore clothing I associated with the 1930s – Oxford bags, a long raincoat and a trilby hat. What really mystified me at the time was wondering how he got in, for all the doors were locked. I called out "Good morning. I'm afraid we are not open until tomorrow, but can I help?" He glanced at me, smiled and simply disappeared, just like that, vanished. There was nothing frightening about him at all, just puzzling.'

This was not the only occasion when the stranger was seen. He has been witnessed by a number of people, both stallholders and customers, who always provide a matching description of the figure. He has become known as 'Old Thorndyke', although Vicki Davies, the wife of the manager, was unable to offer any special reason. 'I merely termed him "old", because he has been seen so many times. He isn't really old, but looks like a chap of about thirty.'

It seems that when the brewers occupied the building, one of the most dedicated young executives was 'a real work acoholic' who let it be known that even if Mackesons closed down, he would never leave. He couldn't, it was his life. He

The Malthouse

was so dedicated to his work that when his employers did finally leave, he hanged himself from the stairway, it is said. The man's name was thought to be Albert Thorndike.

The local television company, TVS, made a documentary item about 'Old Albert' some years ago. During filming an electrician reported seeing the mysterious figure walking slowly up the stairs. 'I thought he was about to ask for a cup of tea from the shop there,' he said, 'but just as he reached the top landing, he vanished.'

John Mitchell, a former stallholder who now runs his own shop nearby, told me of an interesting poltergeist incident he witnessed a few years ago. One Thursday evening at about four o'clock, he went in to check his display of military memorablia, only to find that the order had been completely reversed. 'Last war stuff was in the front and older souvenirs placed at the back. Just as I was about to start rearranging the display, a china saucer rose from the top of a counter and landed on a cabinet a couple of feet away, smashing a glass dome in the process!'

HYTHE

Saltwood Castle

ORIGINALLY a Norman castle, Saltwood was rebuilt in 1160 and ten years later four knights left here to assassinate Thomas a Becket. The building was later given to Henry VIII by Cranmer, but fell into a ruinous state, only being saved from complete destruction in Victorian times.

It is now the home of the Clark family. It was Alan Clark MP, the former Defence Minister, who admitted that his mother found the cost of maintenance there was too high for her, so passed on the ownership to him in 1971. Alan's wife Jane told me early in 1998 that she and several guests have seen the ghostly monk that frequents one of the bedrooms.

As a young boy Alan suffered a frightening experience in front of the black, weathered steps of the impressive 14th century gatehouse, and he is convinced that someone is buried there. However he is unable to see the sense in investigating 'by digging up some old bones'. His philosphy is 'let the dead rest in peace'.

A second figure has been seen in the library, and some describe it as being that of a woman in grey clothing. As far as proof is concerned, Mr Clark needs none. 'I have experienced too much of the supernatural to waste my time with sceptics, and as I said earlier, there is no need, in my view, to disturb the dead.'

IDE HILL

SOUTH of Brasted, a number of motorists have experienced some danger-ous and mystifying incidents when passing through Ide Hill, the wood owned by The National Trust.

At 11.30 one night in 1976, a woman driving north passed the entrance drive to Chains Farm and slowed for the bend in the road when she spotted a young lad in motorcycle gear, holding a rucksack on his arm, stooping as if to get into a car. She braked quickly, but it was too late and her car bonnet hit the boy who appeared to have been knocked under the vehicle.

Shaking and trembling, the driver got out to see what she could do – but there was nothing to be seen. No body, no rucksack and not even a dent on the car. Not believing that the boy could simply have got up and walked away, the woman searched for the victim but finally gave up and reported the incident to a police station. She was advised to 'try and forget it'.

'This sort of incident is not unique to that part of the road,' said the sergeant in charge of Sevenoaks police station. 'A young lad who had crashed his bike in the wood a couple of years before was about to be picked up by a passing motorist, when he was knocked down by another speeding car and killed out-right. Believe me', he added, 'we are still looking for that killer who failed to stop and report the acci-dent.'

KEMSING

Church of
St Mary the Virgin

THIS small and beautiful village surrounds St Edith's Well, named after Edith, daughter of King Edgar the Peaceful, and Lady Wulfrith, born in Kemsing in AD 961.

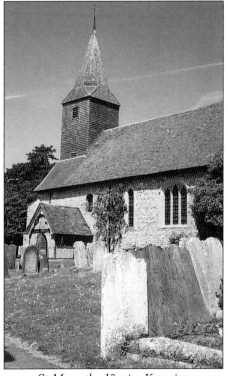

St Mary the Virgin, Kemsing

In 1988 members of the Gravesend Parapsychology Research Group carried out an investigation project in the local cemetery, hoping to record or actually witness some of the phenomena that had been reported over the years, right up to the current time. Shortly after midnight a sound 'similar to that of hoof-beats' was heard by one of the team, who also saw a faint light moving across the grass towards the church. The group then noticed that the building was illuminated from within, yet it had been locked earlier by the vicar who had told them that the church was empty.

A few weeks later a group from London carried out a further vigil and was able to confirm the same supernatural mystery, without achieving any satisfactory explanation.

KINGSDOWN

Old Stairs Bay

S OME two miles to the east of Oxney Bottom is the small community of Kingsdown, comprising a thriving holiday park and scout camp, overlooking Old Stairs Bay. It is an area of considerable archaeological interest with a number of Stone Age sites, Barrows Hill with its tumuli and Barrow Mount.

Within the last six years the 'Blue Lady of Romney Codd' has made a welcome return, walking the cliff path through the camp above Undercliff Road

The view towards Kingsdown

42

and vanishing at a gateway at the recently built fence of Kingsdown House. This is one of the most unusual haunts, for the woman in question has been heard to moan as she is seen again a few yards away on the path leading to the village, and sometimes she is spotted drinking from a small spring on her route.

The title 'Blue Lady' derives from the colour of her gown, which shimmers as she walks, and 'Romney Codd' is thought to be the name of a long lost village, once situated in a valley behind Kingsdown, perhaps in the region of Knight Bottom. Her visitations at one time were fairly regular, according to author Paul Harris, but more associated with storms or wrecks. Her identity remains unknown, as does the cause of her haunting

KNOCKHOLT

Harrow Inn

TINA Ashby, the tenant who took over here with her husband John in 1996, told me that this 400-year-old tavern has a long reputation of being haunted by two ghosts, a man and a woman. The male figure is that of a highwayman, but seen these days only as a long gauntlet, according to the barmaid, Carole Jackson. It is believed that it was this character, fully visible in earlier days, who was the inspiration for Alfred Noye's poem *The Highwayman.*

He robbed the pub but was caught, placed in the cellars (part of which now forms the men's lavatory) and taken out the following day to be hanged and placed in a gibbet on the crossroads a few yards from the pub.

John is reluctant to accept that ghosts exist, but is unable to explain a recent problem in the spillage area in which a barrel was lifted, by some unseen force or person, over several others and placed on its end on the floor.

The female figure has been witnessed quite recently by Tina and her twenty one-year-old daughter, in the front doorway, shortly before closing time. On the first occasion, a Sunday in October 1997, Tina suddenly felt a remarkable drop in temperature, and thinking that her husband had left the main door open, asked him to close it. But it was already shut and she could see, standing in the doorway, the figure of a woman in a black cloak. 'I was still shivering from the cold,' Tina told me, 'when it just faded away.'

This was, perhaps, the same figure that a friend of mine saw in 1980, although not as a woman in a black cloak but 'rather as the shadowy figure of a tramp in a large but very dark coat, standing in the doorway just at closing time'. Several others in the pub at the time also noticed the creepy figure.

LAMBERHURST

The Chequers

THIS inn is on the main London to Hastings road, practically in the centre of Lamberhurst and once within the borders of Sussex. It was owned from the 1500s to the late 18th century by the Thomas family of Coggers Hall and one of the phantoms that haunts the ancient building may well be a member of the family. Known as the 'Woman in Red', the ghost has been reported quite recently, and quite frequently, but only by female members of the staff and visitors. One of the younger members of the team went into the dining room one morning with breakfast for a guest and was surprised to see the figure of a woman wearing a long burgundy coloured gown, looking out of the window. She turned to face the girl only to vanish in front of her.

Local historian Ian Peters heard evidence from a previous landlady that once she had heard footsteps going up the stairs, but was assured by her husband that there had been no-one to account for the sound. On another night she had placed all the chairs on the tables prior to washing the floor, switched off all the lights and gone into the next room, but within half a minute of sitting down she saw the vague figure of a woman in a wine coloured dress pass the doorway. Within seconds there was such a lot of noise in the empty room that

The Chequers, Lamberhurst

44

she dashed in, only to find that all the chairs were carefully placed back in their former places, on the floor; of the woman there was no trace.

More specific phenomena affects Room Four. It is often so cold, despite the heating, that guests have been known to request extra blankets. One refused to spend another night in the hotel because of all the 'tappings' he had heard, whilst another had the alarming experience of feeling that 'an invisible someone or something' had been trying to get into bed with him. A former barmaid, Ruby Jones, told of the experience she had when sitting at the till in the main bar. It was about 11.30pm, and although the bar was officially closed, there were several customers still chatting in the saloon. The public bar was completely empty. Suddenly a woman with 'longish dark hair parted in the middle, and wearing a black top with a white collar', peered around the corner of the dividing door and withdrew. No-one fitting that description was in the hotel that night.

Court Lodge

LYNN Smith, a milk recorder who works in Mayfield, was one of many witnesses to a phantom car that has been seen on the road near Bewl Bridge. It was early one morning, late in 1997, that she was approaching a particularly bad corner in her car when she saw headlights coming rapidly down the hill towards her. She slowed down and pulled in to the hedgerow to let the other vehicle pass but, despite the lights and the sound of a car engine, there was nothing to be seen; the road was empty. At the precise moment when the invisible vehicle would be abreast of her, the audio cassette Lynn was listening to shot out of the player.

This was not her first experience of the paranormal. Shortly after moving into a flat at Court Lodge, one of the three manor houses in the village, she was plagued by falling curtains and by the heavy iron doors of her large old cooker opening suddenly of their own accord.

Originally Lynn had put up her curtains with a length of wire hooked at each end, but at every attempt to hang them the curtains fell down. Finally she decided to use curtain rods with rings. No sooner was this in place than the rod, complete with curtains, collapsed, and she was forced to nail the curtains to the wall.

Horse and Groom Cottage

THIS attractive private house was, until fairly recently, a pub with the same name, and it is from the experiences of a former landlord, and some pre-

Horse and Groom Cottage

vious customers, together with the researches of Ian Peters, that the incidents in the original tavern establish this as another genuine haunted site.

One evening the shadow of a woman and a small child were seen by a member of the staff, standing in the kitchen, and a former regular, Peter Harmer, commented, 'I'm glad to see that the woman and the kid are back', yet neither the landlord nor other staff members were able to see the couple.

Bernard Bryant, one of the customers before the pub reverted to private use, recalls when he and a group of friends were in the left hand bar at a time when the landlord and his wife were away. Suddenly they heard the sound of someone running around in the empty rooms upstairs. What was more peculiar was the sound of childish giggles coming, it seems, from the fireplace, although none of the witnesses felt bold enough to investigate.

Quizzed on his return, Adrian Kirkman, the landlord, said the sounds had come from the pub ghosts, and he admitted that on more than one occasion overnight guests had been tipped out of their beds by something unseen in one of the rooms. According to historian John Moon the 'lady ghost of the tavern' cannot belong to a period earlier than 1710, because the wall that she was seen to walk through on the stairs, and where once there was a doorway, was built in that year, when the building was converted from a leather workshop.

Lindridge Place

S HORTLY before Christmas 1986, Bernard Bryant, the gardener at this delightful 16th century property, was working in the grounds whilst the

Lindridge Place Farm

owners, Grahame and Sheila Dutch were away on holiday, when he decided to take a break and make himself a pot of tea. As he opened the back door to the kitchen, the family dog, a friendly labrador, began to bark and implied by his 'fussing about' that something needed attention in another room. Bernard followed as the dog lead him to the door of the main hall, where the animal became agitated. Bernard cautiously opened the door and was shocked to see a woman leaning against the chimney breast of the inglenook fireplace. Assuming it was an unexpected guest, he greeted the unknown visitor only to see her gradually fade away in front of him. Rather than risk upsetting his employer's festivities over the holiday period, he made no mention of the unusual incident until well into the New Year, and was pleasantly surprised to realise that they were not at all concerned or worried about the haunting. In fact they rather welcomed the idea of 'having a sort of guardian in the house'.

Two years later, whilst in the kitchen, Mr Dutch heard footsteps approaching the landing at the top of the stairs and then 'an almighty crash as if a massive pile of crockery had been thrown down'. He dashed out, to find no explanation or cause for the supposedly horrifying smash.

Before the Dutch family occupied the building it had been a restaurant, and they discovered a wall cupboard near the stairs to be full of crockery. But this was still firmly fixed.

Some days later Mr Dutch mentioned the phenomenal incidents to a medical friend and described the ghost seen by the gardener as wearing riding breeches and a 17th century frock coat. The reply was totally unexpected. 'Why that's Miss Japp!' This rather unusual woman, who had owned the property before the Second World War, was found dead in the lavatory at the top of the stairs, next to the crockery cupboard.

No really startling incidents have been experienced since Miss Japp made her presence known, except that the smell of pipe tobacco occurs occasionally and small objects, such as silver napkin rings disappear suddenly, only to reappear days later. One day the family found the living room strewn with hops and grain, when neither was available.

Windmill Cottage

MOST guide books and some visitors associate Lamberhurst solely with the nearby 14th century Scotney Castle, with its doubtful tale of a ghostly customs officer being drowned in the moat and knocking on the front door of the ruined tower. Admittedly a maid did meet her death there, which caused problems as to which county, Sussex or Kent, would provide a coroner, for at the time the village was divided by the county boundary. When, in 1894, the villagers realised the rates were considerably lower in Kent, they decided that the whole community should be maintained by the northern county. Windmill Cottage, formerly worker's cottages, is said to be haunted by Granny Ralphs, a former tenant, who died in 1918.

In the 1980s Adrian Harland, son of the then owners, was awoken suddenly one night by an almighty crash. He looked around his bedroom and realised that his alarm clock, originally on the top of a chest of drawers beside his bed, had been thrown across the room to smash against the far wall with such force that it was shattered into several pieces, and had badly dented the plaster. When he told his mother about 'the flying clock', he was surprised to learn that she had previously seen the figure of an elderly woman wearing a long black dress and a large black hat with a prominent hat pin, standing at the foot of the bed.

The mysterious ghostly female remained for only a few seconds before disappearing, but surprisingly, she returned a few nights later, to stand at the head of the bed; this time she was hatless, and her hair was in a bun. The figure was holding a ball of wool in her hand and seemed to be knitting. Mrs Harland went to approach her but the image faded away. The phantom was identified by Delsey Playfoot, a relative and neighbour, who remembered seeing Granny Ralphs through the window, when she went to school.

LENHAM

Chilston Park Hotel

ACCORDING to the *Evening Standard*, this 18th century manor house provides a 'real traditional ambience highlighted by the bizarre mass of antiques'. Yet no mention was made of the ghost seen there by a number of people, staff and visitors alike. Claire Tierney, one of the team that caters for the comfort of guests, saw the apparition during the summer of 1997.

'I was walking up the staircase', she told me, 'and noticed someone in one of the mirrors that border the stairs. I thought that it was one of my colleagues, for all the staff wear authentic 18th century costume, and the man in the mirror was in full footman's livery. I turned to greet him, but there was no-one there, although when turning back to the glass, the image was still visible.' Sue, another member of staff, confirmed that the footman had been seen on a number of occasions.

LYDD

Ladson Lodge

BUILT in about 1650 and once part of a pub, Ladson Lodge is now home to Jilly Walker, her two sons, a dog and an invisible entity. On the day she moved in, early in 1998, her eldest son, twenty two-years-old, wondered who the 'someone' was who was walking across one of the empty rooms upstairs. Shortly afterwards, his nineteen-year-old brother heard the same noise, together with that of a child coughing.

'Although the sounds have continued, spasmodically, the warm friendly atmosphere of the place makes us feel really quite comfortable,' Jilly said. 'I asked the estate agent about the property's history and was told that some years ago part of the house had been badly burnt and a child's toy boat had been discovered in the fireplace during the renovation.' Jilly added: 'We naturally assume that it belonged to the youngster who died from the affects of the fire.'

One night when she was lying in bed waiting for the return of her son from Tunbridge Wells, she heard his car arrive, but as it came to a halt, she felt a sudden slap on her leg as if her ghostly companion had said, in effect, 'he's back, wake up!' The general feeling about the unseen resident is that she is a kind woman perhaps associated with the child who, according to Michael Jack, the local dowser, probably died in 1817, although the footsteps are 'definitely those of a man'.

Sky-Trek Airport

During the early 1950s a small private airfield was built for Silver City between the smuggling village of Lydd, and Greatstone-on-Sea. It is now owned by Jonathan Gordon who established Sky Trek Airlines here in June 1997. Alan Harradine, the airline's maintenance manager, confirmed that up to a few years ago a number of paranormal incidents had been experienced in the airport building, all associated with the sudden and totally unexpected death of Jack Dartford in the late 1950s. To prevent embarrasment I have used a pseudonym for the victim.

Jack was one of the team of loaders dealing with the transportation of freight on and off the cargo aircraft, a Bristol Freighter, and about 6pm one evening in October 1957 or 1958, when handling the last flight, on the last day of the weekly run, he suddenly felt ill. 'We took him into the cabin, and sat him down, but only minutes later he was dead,' Alan told me. 'We never found out the cause.'

From then on, for many months, weird things would happen in areas connected with Jack. Lavatories would flush, doors would open and close themselves, 'we would hear footsteps in the loading shed when it was empty, and a number of small objects would be found to have moved or just vanished. Ashtrays, glasses and empty bottles would disappear and then be rediscovered. It was all rather funny, really,' Alan said. 'We haven't experienced anything now for about eight years, or at least nothing has been reported. But one never knows. Jack was such a dedicated worker and thoroughly enjoyed his time here.'

Some ten miles to the north east lies the site of another small airport at Lympne, now forming part of an industrial estate. In July 1980 Pauline Kane of Folkestone was due to participate in a parachute jump with Captain Alex Black and a group of friends. However Pauline suddenly saw 'a vision' of her father in the clouds surrounding the plane, and heard her his voice warn her not to jump. Having been very close to him, and nursed him until he died, Pauline, who had heard her father's footsteps in her home weeks after his funeral, accepted the warning and decided not to complete the jump. On Wednesday July 2 an EP9 Prospector aircraft, piloted by Alex, left with the group of five parachutists for a routine flight and combined jump, but only minutes after take off, the plane crashed in a field, a few yards from Lydd, and all the occupants were killed.

Pauline Kane has not experienced any further phenomena and has moved away from the region. Some still wonder however, whether it was this incident that also affected, in some way, the nearby Lydd Airport.

MAIDSTONE

Blue Bell Hill

O N Friday November 19, 1965, a Ford Cortina containing four young women crashed head-on with an oncoming Jaguar driven by a young man travelling with his companion. Reports vary as to the result of the appalling accident. Some say that Judith Linham of Rochester, who was due to be married the next day, was killed outright, that one passenger died later in hospital and a third in the ambulance. Other records show that the driver, Susan Down, lived for five days after the crash, while Judith died the day following the collision. The fatally injured passenger was Patricia Ferguson. Both reports agree that the sole survivor was Gillian Birchet, who was unable to talk about the tragedy and has never spoken of it since.

The site of the accident is a few yards from a pedestrian bridge over the Old Chatham Road, one of the stretches of the A229 north of Maidstone. To the south lie the ancient ruins of Kit's Coty House, an iron age burial chamber, and the Lower Bell public house. A few yards to the north is Blue Bell Hill. In 1974 taxi driver Maurice Goodenough, from Rochester, claimed that late one night in July, a young girl standing at the bus stop only a few feet away from the accident site, jumped out in front of his vehicle, and being unable to stop in time, he knocked her down. He picked up the body, placed it on the side of the road, covered it with his car blanket and, as he was unable to stop other

Aftermath of the crash on Blue Bell Hill in 1965

51

Blue Bell Hill, 1978

vehicles, drove to Maidstone to report the matter. The police found nothing but the sodden blanket.

The description of the girl resembled none of the wedding party, for Maurice saw 'a girl of about ten, wearing a white blouse, white ankle socks and a skirt, who had several cuts to her head and knees'.

There have been a number of similarly strange incidents in exactly the same area. One of the most recent to be recorded was that of Ian Sharpe who told Maidstone Police of a young girl who suddenly appeared in front of his car on November 10, 1992. He returned to the site with a number of police officers, but as before, nothing was found.

It was during the latter half of the 1960s that an increasing number of reports were being received about a young girl seen standing waiting at the bus stop, in the rain, always at about 11pm, hitching a ride to either Maidstone or Rochester, depending on the source. She would get into a car and sit in the back, said the motorists who had stopped for the girl, but on arriving at the address given she had vanished and the response from the 'mother' was 'It can't be my daughter, she was killed in November 1965'.

Linked with the BBC's Radio Kent and the Kent Messenger Group, I issued a challenge to anyone who could produce a genuine witness of the phantom hitch-hiker, but received only one applicant hoping for the £100 reward. He was, I fear, intoxicated at the time.

During the last thirty years more than thirty five motorists claim to have had 'close encounters with the ghost' and the police now accept the incidents involve phantoms. Roger Grim, one of the police officers on duty during a recent case in which a motorist claimed to have hit a young girl on Blue Bell Hill, said: 'Our report concludes that he hit a ghost.'

Despite the continuing and thorough investigations by Sean Tudor of Maidstone, who has spent several years researching and recording the phantom hitch-hiker, reports now concentrate more on the single 'jaywalker' rather than the hitch-hiking girl. Sean told me that Maidstone is probably one of the only police stations to make an official log of the existence of such ghostly incidents. He feels, however, that it is more than likely there are two spectres that frequent the scene. One witness recently described a 'horrible old hag with a ghastly evil face' jumping out in front of his lorry, whilst others still see the 'young girl of about twenty'.

One aspect could be the general disturbance of the area, for when the Dover motorway was being built, numerous reports were made of 'ghostly Roman soldiers' being spotted near the Roman burial site, and when the dual carriageway construction was under way here, at Blue Bell Hill, the increase in phantom hitch-hiker reports was very noticeable.

Maidstone Hospital

IN the 1970s West Kent General Hospital was equipped with 163 beds but by 1979 it had also gained the sound of an invisible crying ghost.

The building dates from the 18th century and has been so modified that there is little likelihood of being able to trace the identity of the unseen woman whose pitiful cries affect one specific ward, usually at night.

One of the most recent reports of the sobbings was made by a Mr Day, a charge nurse on night duty. 'The woman sounds completely heartbroken,' he said. 'It really is rather distressing, especially as there is absolutely nothing that we can do to ease her troubles. We did contact a priest and the hospital padre, but, so far, without success.'

The staff remain puzzled and upset, but accept that it is impossible to treat an invisible patient.

Museum and Art Gallery

THIS fascinating museum and art centre is housed in the old Chillington Manor House and is affected by a most unusual 'emanation', issuing from an oil painting. The picture is that of a gypsy girl, and is displayed among many others in the Baxter Print Room.

I spoke to Veronica Tonge, keeper of the Fine Art Collection, in May 1998, and learnt that although no-one has ever reported seeing or hearing anything of a paranormal nature, there have been fairly regular comments concerning the 'peculiar waves of some invisible force coming specifically from that picture'. It is not clear who was the artist or the title of the subject.

For some ten years during the 1970s and early 1980s, I tutored in the Adult Education Centre next to the Museum, and during breaks would visit the Art Gallery for a chat with the curator. He told me even then that the weird feeling in the area surrounding the picture was often reported. It was simply mysterious. One possible explanation that has been offered is that in the minds of some visitors there is an association of legendary psychic powers with the gypsy race, the Romanies. But who can tell?

Inexplicable footsteps have also been heard by members of the staff coming down the main staircase, but they fade away when nearing the last step.

MARGATE

Dreamland Fun Park

THIS twenty acre entertainment area practically adjoinins the sea front, and was once home to Britain's oldest wooden roller coaster (sold in 1998 to Mexico). In the area of the Stowaway River Ride in June 1997, London Weekend Television filmed me for an episode in the *Strange But True* series hosted by Michael Aspel, after security staff reported strange happenings and called for an investigation.

Dreamland, close to the site of the weight guesser's kiosk

The main complaint had been of the sound of mysterious and unaccountable footsteps, 'quite loud', together with 'constant bouts of whispering, and the general feeling of being watched.' One of the most noteworthy occasions was when Mick with Frank Buckery were putting up Christmas decorations around the entrance. Suddenly, and for no reason, they both felt intense and spine-chilling cold, and heard the sound of an invisible walker striding around the empty arena.

David Bill, the operations manager, said that although female staff were willing to enter the area at night, it was difficult to persuade any of the male security officers to check out the Stowaway River Ride, which was sited in the former Bali Hi pub cellars. The gloomy and creepy atmosphere created by plastic skeletons glowing with phosphorescence, and pools of dark swirling water, was not the ideal place in which to hang around, especially at night.

After some hours of interviewing and carrying out investigation, using various electronic response units, no satisfactory explanation could be found.

The Stowaway River Ride area is where, according to local history, a horrible murder had occurred nearly a century ago. The killer, known as 'Margate's Strong Man' had met a woman at the roller skating rink but, failing to persuade her to comply with his desires, had strangled her and thrown her body into the nearby gardens. He was later hanged for the crime.

Seven years earlier I had been called to investigate a more substantial haunting at Dreamland Fun Park in which the figure of a former stallholder had been seen by a couple of security guards. John Hiscock, one of the guards, had been locking up with Trevor Naylor one night when they saw 'Old Henry', the weight guesser, walk around a corner of the arcade and 'just vanish'.

'He was not normally around at that time of night, so we went to find him,' John said. 'But he was nowhere to be found.' Both the men were shocked the next day to learn that Henry had been found dead in his one room flat in the

The weight guesser's kiosk

town, on the day that the new owners of Dreamland, Bembom Brothers, signed the transfer documents. The stallholder had been dead for some hours when his shade was witnessed by the security team.

Over the years he had been offering his skill at guessing the weight of visitors, but had gained a bit of a reputation as 'a naughty feeler'. On searching the area of his kiosk, I found a couple of the rings that he gave to customers whose weight he guessed incorrectly, and later offered one to a psychometrist who told me, after holding the ring for a few seconds: 'This was one of several rings owned by a short, rather dumpy man, who would wear a long coat and a hat and had an unfortunate, rather disgusting manner with the girls. I don't like the feel of it.' The description matched that of Henry. His figure has not been seen since.

Theatre Royal

MANY of England's theatres are genuinely haunted and one of the most reliable cases in Kent is the former 'home' of Sarah Thorne, the founder of the theatrical company. The theatre, Britain's second oldest, has attracted a lot of attention from scientists such as Dr ARG Owen of Cambridge and members of the Association for the Scientific Study of Anamolous Phenomena, personalities in the shape of Ena Twigg, one of the country's most respected mediums, and of course the theatrical world itself including Macqueen Pope, who saw a ghost near the orchestra pit and assumed it to be of an actor who killed himself by jumping from one of the boxes early in the 20th century. In more recent times a 'semi-transparent object' has been witnessed gliding across the floor of the stage, and the sounds of an invisible 'someone' have been heard walking in the same locality when the theatre was empty except for maintenance staff.

Theatre Royal, Margate

Because of the interest in the haunting as a genuine example of the paranormal, members of the respected Ghost Club and later others from a local research group have both held all night vigils in the building. 'A ball of light' was captured by a camcorder 'hovering on the centre stage when all the others had been extinguished', but this mysterious light has often been observed by a number of independent witnesses. Some members of the society that visited the old property in May 1996 admitted that they had sensed 'someone in one of the boxes' and on one occasion a member had felt an unseen hand push him in the back.

A relative of mine attended a lecture in the theatre shortly after the celebrations of the theatre's 210 years of existence, and as a former professional actress, asked permission to wander around the building during a coffee break. On returning she told of feeling a strong presence in one specific box

Sarah Thorne, founder of Maidstone's theatrical company

and on indicating the site was told that that was where Sarah Thorne had been seen several times, but it was also thought to be from where the suicide jumped to his death.

NEWINGTON

George Inn

A FEW miles from Sittingbourne is the larger of the two Newingtons, the other is near Folkestone, but it is this one, practically linked with Rainham, that has associations with the Devil. It is said that his footprint can be seen in a stone at the entrance to the church of St Mary the Virgin.

The village was also once a major section of the Newington Lucies estate, complete with its own manor house and convent, to combat, no doubt, the interest expressed by The Evil One.

In 1978 new tenants moved into The George in the High Street but within a few months realised that not only had they taken on a number of enthusiastic regular customers, but also, it seems, a resident ghost. Landlady Rosemary Martin was working in the kitchen one day, but began to feel uneasy. 'Somebody was watching me,' she told author Guy Lyon Playfair, who specialises in the paranormal field, in 1980. 'But it was rather vague. When I turned round, all I saw was a sort of grey hooded shadow, but it had no specific features.'

Her husband Peter was disappointed that he had noticed nothing. However, their daughter Helen, then aged five, when being tucked up in bed that night, wanted to know from her mother who was the man 'with a dress on and a sort of a hood'. The child was later able to draw a rough sketch of the figure, which showed the outline of a monk's habit complete with corded belt and a hood.

Only a few days later one of the regulars, standing at the bar, suddenly stared at Rosemary and asked, somewhat tremulously: 'Who is the monk standing behind you?' Rosemary turned to see the vague shape fade away.

The haunting experienced now is merely an occasional example of poltergeist phenomena in which plates and knives have been swept from table tops, a picture taken down from one wall and propped up against another, a hand mirror found face down on the kitchen floor, and the movement of glasses and bottles.

Lance Morgan, a former regular customer, told a researcher in 1992 that he was with some friends in the saloon, the original public bar, when a door at the far end of the room opened and footsteps were heard walking towards the corridor leading to the outside lavatory, but there was nothing to account for the sound. Cyril Harris, the landlord at the time, suggested that the invisible walker could have been associated with the murdered nun. The legend responsible for that belief was that a young sister from Newington Convent was discovered in an affair with a monk He was put to death and the nun was bricked up alive in what is now the cellar of The George.

NEW ROMNEY

New Inn

NEW Romney dates from the 11th century and, like Hythe, formed one of the original Cinque Ports. Old Romney became stranded well inland as a result of the changing coast line and the varying routes of the river Rother.

By the 14th century the town had grown in size and importance, and one of the taverns, the New Inn, became a popular watering hole for residents, visitors, travellers, smugglers – and now tourists interested in the intriguing tales of Dr Syn and the marshes.

Dr Syn, alias The Scarecrow, was a fictional parson, created by Russell

Thorndike, who led a group of smugglers through and around the Romney Marsh area.

One morning some 200 years ago, a young woman named Elizabeth was found hanging from the inn's main staircase. No explanation has ever been discovered or offered for her suicide, but as in so many cases of sudden or inexplicable death, her wraith remains to haunt what was once her home.

A former landlord once saw the figure of a young woman walk silently through the bar. The current tenant, Graham Wright, experienced the most noteworthy incident, in 1996. At about 1am on an August morning he was finishing some work in the kitchen when he noticed a dark figure walk through the passage from the public bar, and approach him. It was, according to Paul Harris, who investigated the case, 'a rather indistinct shape which passed him, but leaving Graham suffering from cold pins and needles'. The feeling was 'strange but certainly not frightening'. The 'visit' was in fact repeated shortly before Paul's arrival, but with the 'shadow' of the phantom being seen alongside that of Graham, by another witness. When Graham turned back he realised that the figure, presumably that of 'Elizabeth', had vanished.

The Old Priory

ON the corner of the High Street and Ashford Road lies an intriguing old building which dates back to 1270. In its front sector is a craft and novelty shop, and in the portion facing the recreation ground is Dave Picott's upholstery workshop, which covers the site of the church associated with this old priory.

In an excellent book *Ghosts of the Coast* produced in 1996, Paul Harris, who interviewed Dave, tells that although nothing has been seen Dave is convinced that, at times, there is someone watching him. Unexplained sounds of moving objects are heard and 'weird whispering' can be detected in a couple of empty rooms. However there is one incident that Dave will never forget. It occurred one night when he was working late. Suddenly he noticed the sound of footsteps approaching, 'but whatever it was, a presence, an entity, or whatever' continued to walk straight through him. 'It was cold and petrifying,' was his comment.

This was an extraordinary coincidence, for in 1977 I was persuaded by members of my evening class in the Adult Education Centre to arrange a 'vigil' for the group, to investigate the haunting known to exist in the building. At that time the front was occupied by an antiques dealer, who told us that he had stock worth some £28,000 in the cellars, and it was for that reason

The Old Priory, New Romney

I arranged for a 24 hour insurance policy to cover the risk to the students, having been told also that the floorboards upstairs 'were a bit dicey'.

The manager of the shop had claimed that his wife had seen two monk-like figures at the top of the stairs on the first landing, but he had seen them as two old women.

During the three hours of our stay, two members of the group, equipped with a tape recorder and a thermometer, heard and recorded an inexplicable tapping that passed them, only inches away. 'It sounded like the noise of a blind man's stick' said one later. 'But what was really incredible was that the temperature dropped by eight degrees in the twenty seconds of the walk'. The tapping, or clicking, had started at the doorway of the empty room, only to cease on reaching the archway leading to the next room in which a piscina was fitted in one corner. A local historian was later fascinated to learn of our experiences. She said evidence existed that 'five or six people were tortured in that room during the Civil War'.

We had earlier been told by a former secretary of an optician, that she had frequently heard the sound of footsteps ascending the stairway, turning along the corridor past her office and stopping on reaching the 'surgery'. She had been so mystified by the continual visit, which always seemed to be on a Monday evening, that she decided to see what would happen if she waited at the top of the stairs to greet the unseen patient. Like Dave, some twenty years later, when the footsteps went right through her, she felt as if her whole body had been dropped into liquid ice. 'But after only a couple of seconds on hearing the tread continue along the corridor behind me, I felt warm again. It really was quite weird,' she said.

NORTHFLEET

Ye Olde Leathern Bottel

EARLY in 1978 I was asked by the brewers, Trumans, to carry out research into the haunting of this attractive pub situated on the Dover Road, and found what was possibly a case of a ghost of the living.

Janet and Barry Mason, the landlords at the time, believed that the house was formed from three farm cottages, which in the 16th century was converted into an inn. In September 1976, shortly after moving in, they noticed that the door to the gentleman's toilet would open and close of its own accord and, despite attention from a carpenter, it continued for several months, until it stopped as inexplicably as it started.

Then, the peculiar 'phase' transferred to another door at the top of the stairs leading to the Mason's flat. 'You could hear the sound of the hooks on the door shaking,' Janet told me. 'It was a bit un-nerving for a time. Eventually the problem ceased but toilet items from the bathroom were moved or disappeared completely.' Some of the builder's equipment was also shifted about, causing many hours of wasted time searching for them, before having to accept that, sometimes, replacements had to be purchased. The workmen were considerably annoyed when, returning with new items, they found the missing tools, such as a plumb line, a level and several chisels, 'displayed' on the floor of the bathroom.

The more specific haunting however was experienced one night early in 1977 when Janet, three friends and two of the bar staff were sitting chatting in the lounge. The front door had been locked some minutes earlier. Suddenly Janet glanced up to see the figure of a woman with dark brown hair moving rapidly towards the bar but then vanish from sight behind one of the pillars. The group searched the whole of the ground floor but found no trace of the visitor. 'She had a pink face and was wearing a greyish blue fitted sleeve cardigan, Janet said. 'Initially we thought she was a customer who had been accidentally locked in, but she wasn't. She had simply disappeared.'

A few weeks later Paul, a new member of the staff, received confirmation from a regular customer, that the apparition of a young man with long fair hair seen walking towards the kitchen wall before disappearing, had been seen a little while earlier by himself and other customers. They too, thought it was the figure of some-one accidentally locked in.

Yet another visitation was of 'a misty shape like a negative of a photo' reported by Sylvia, a member of the staff, who had also seen the ghostly young man, wearing a long brown coat near the kitchen wall.

Janet feels that the three figures are merely 'reminders of past occupants of the old original cottages,' but Barry, who had seen nothing untoward but felt he had been watched on every occasion by 'an unseen something', thought that they may well be 'phantasms of the living – customers who are still alive but have moved away and can only visualise themselves in their favourite pub'.

There is a classic case of such a haunting of an Inn in the Old Kent Road, London, where the tenant was seen, even though she had retired and moved about fifteen miles away, standing in the cellars with her arms folded, looking at the new landlord opening one of the barrels. Her appearance lasted for only about half a minute, but when the old lady read about the incident in her local paper, she visited the pub to assure 'the new people and all and sundry that she was no blooming ghost, but very much alive, and would be for some time yet.'

OTFORD

Otford Palace

THE ruins of Otford Palace seem more to house pigeons than reminders of the notorious and curious Elizabeth Barton.

A maidservant of Thomas Cobb, she was born in 1506 in Aldington, but when nineteen-years-old developed what was probably epilepsy or the more puzzling form, temporal lobe epilepsy. During her 'absences' Elizabeth acquired the ability to know what was happening in other locations, a sort of clairvoyance, combined in certain instances, with premonition. She found herself in trouble when she was persuaded by the church to claim that Henry VIII's marriage to Anne Boleyn was not recognised by God, and she was eventually tried, here, in Otford Palace, where she was found guilty of treason. In April 1534 she was taken to Tyburn to be hanged. Cobbs Hall and the ruined chapel in Street, where she assured her supporters that she would be healed of her afflictions, have become sites for pilgrims anxious to visit places associated with the 'Holy Maid of Kent', as she was known.

In 1978 I visited the palace and discussed the history of the ruin with a visiting council executive. He was there to check on a recent report of 'a mysteri ous figure of a young woman seen strolling round the south side of the tower, who vanished when spoken to'. She has been described as wearing a long blue or grey gown and has her head bowed, as if in sorrow. Could this young woman be the Holy Maid I wonder?

OXNEY BOTTOM

A258

IN the late 1970s I was told by an archaeologist attached to Dover Town Council of the strange incidents at Oxney Bottom, where for no apparent reason, drivers heading north on the Dover-Deal road are likely to land up in a field on the left, on the dangerous S-bend opposite woods. Neither excessive speed nor bad weather were ever the cause.

Several explanations have been offered for the many crashes, often fatal, that occur there. One unusual answer that was fully researched, was that a stream under the road at the specific location, travelling to or from the remains of St Nicholas's Church in the woods, was some form of evil affecting drivers. The route of this was actually realigned after a major accident, but it seems that the problem has not yet been fully cured, for the report of another inexplicable crash has been recorded, together with the appearance of 'a grey lady'. According to Paul Harris, a recent coach party witnessed the wraith of a woman in grey cross the path of the vehicle which was on its way to Walmer Castle. The driver slammed on the brakes, but 'had actually passed through the spectral shade' by the time the coach stopped. As before, no sign or sight of the assumed victim could be found.

Sometime in 1976 I drove to the site but was unable to proceed much further along the drive to the ruins, or to Oxney Court, mainly because of the many warnings to keep out displayed on the trees bordering the access. Also though, I was affected by a distinct feeling of extreme sadness, despondency, even potential horror. One of the phantoms that passes along that driveway, it is said, is the son of an innkeeper from Deal who was hanged as a highwayman on a gibbet at the side of the road.

PEMBURY

Pembury Hospital

WHEN compiling *Ghosts of Today* I was assured by an executive in the nursing profession that 'practically every English hospital is haunted' and she went on to list some of those known personally to her. Many were outside my remit, they were too old for inclusion, but I was able to provide details of some twenty five, giving, I felt, a reasonable selection.

Hoping to find more modern examples, I contacted Pembury Hospital on the Tonbridge Road. Many years ago the building was used as a workhouse, complete with a well organised clinic. The area now part of the transport office, in the management block, was an archway into the hospital chapel, where dead and dying patients were brought in by horse and cart.

One night in March 1996, Brian Wells, the transport manager, who had been working late, heard what he thought was a horse neighing. Puzzled, he went into the reception area, but finding nothing to account for the noise, returned to his office. Within minutes, however, he was conscious of the noise of a horse scraping on what sounded like cobblestones, the sound of impatience, sometimes expressed by waiting animals.

The following day he was astounded to learn of the original use of his office, and that many years earlier, a horse bringing in a number of patients, had for some unknown reason, shied, smashing the cart and killing the driver, who is now buried in the grounds. Mr Wells, an author and researcher into the days of the Raj, assured me that up to March 1996 he had no knowledge of the fatal accident, but he is now intent on finding out more of the history of the old building.

Old Soar Manor

PLAXTOL

Old Soar Manor

THE remains of this late 15th century knight's manor house consist of a two-storey solar and a small chapel, and although the haunting of Old Soar is far from impressive, it is still reported by the occasional visitor.

The cause of odd incidents encountered at the manor is, it is said, a suicide in the 18th century. After being raped by a priest, a dairy maid from the manor, realising that she was pregnant, had hanged herself in the chapel, the site of her attack.

The haunting takes the form of footsteps pacing the floor of the empty room and the shock of 'suddenly feeling intensely cold' at a bend of the stairway to the upper floor. One of the local farm workers who, years ago slept in the chapel to guard the farm produce that was stored there, often heard the sound of 'the invisible walker', and at times, sensed someone 'very, very unhappy' watching him, but he also told of hearing organ music, but was unable to locate the source. This was confirmed by a colleague who occasionally joined him as an overnight guard.

In 1973 the custodian was told by a visitor, who claimed to be clairvoyant, that she had seen the figure of a priest in a black cloak, bending over the piscina, and on returning with a friend shortly afterwards, was nearly overcome by the 'cold spot on the stairs'.

Once in 1974, just as she was clearing up prior to closing for the day, Miss Charlesworth, the custodian at the time, glanced into the chapel and was puzzled to see a dark cloak hanging on the wall adjoining the stairs. She was about to remove it, when she heard the arrival of a couple of visitors, but just before walking downstairs to greet them, she glanced back and realised that the cloak and the water she had noticed in the holy basin, had vanished.

A few days later the figure of a youngish woman wearing a long grey gown with a white apron was seen on the stairs to vanish as she reached the top landing, and in the same year, lights were reported shining out from the empty building. The main switch was found to be turned to the 'off' position when the caretaker was called in to check the mystery.

PLUCKLEY

Black Horse

THIS small village once had the reputation for being the most haunted in the country, with twelve or thirteen active ghosts. When I accompanied a group of students on a ghost hunt in the 1970s, we learnt of three possibly genuine incidents of the paranormal, but since then the number has dropped to the single case of this haunted pub.

Then the trio consisted of a poltergeist at Elvey Park Farm, another here in the Black Horse and, the most interesting to us, the ghostly figure of a woman in red in the churchyard adjoining the tavern. At about 11 o'clock one night, an 18-year-old barmaid, Anne Barham, decided to take a short cut home through the graveyard and, being local and used to all the tales and stories, had no fears of 'any old spectres'.

The Black Horse, Pluckley

However when only a few feet into the area, she noticed that a woman was obviously searching for something and intently looking at the tombstones. 'At first, I wasn't worried,' Anne told us, 'but then I realised that she was wearing red, and felt anyway that it was a bit strange for anyone to be searching a cemetery at that time of night. As I got nearer though, she moved right through two of the upright stones and at that, I'm afraid, I ran back to the pub where John gave me a brandy and arranged to take me home. I'd never drunk spirits before, but he assured me that I needed it.'

John, the chief barman, confirmed what Anne had said and was convinced that she had witnessed the 'mysterious and ghostly woman in red' who is supposed to be looking for the grave of her young daughter.

In October 1996 I was asked by Sky TV, which was producing a series called *Mysteries*, to visit the Black Horse the next day and give my opinion of Anne's experience. Originally, some twenty years earlier, the landlady had shown me her daughter's bedroom where a black coat of hers, which had been hanging at the back of the door, suddenly unhooked itself and flew across the room to land on the bed. The girl at the time, was staying with friends in Bristol.

On arriving at the inn for the filming, I was taken to a tiny room upstairs and, out of breath and suffering from the glare of the floodlights, I was asked what I felt. My reply was, I fear, not what was hoped for, but I learnt later that new owner Laura Gambling and her daughter Joanne had been puzzled by the unaccountable sound of running feet which seemed to originate from that room. Staff member Jackie Oliver told me that whilst polishing horse brasses hanging on the wall near the bar, some unseen hand had touched her shoulder. 'It was just a pat, but I can assure you,' she said, 'there was no-one there'.

RAMSGATE
A253/A256 junction

WHEN the stocks, the pillory and hanging were common forms of punishment, the gibbet at what is now the roundabout junction of the A253 from Canterbury and the A256 from Sandwich, would often contain the rotting corpse of some unfortunate, usually a highwayman or some similar brigand, to act as a deterent to potential criminals. All that remains today seems to be a mere flickering wisp of light that hovers and swings across the junction, like the glow from a huge but unseen lantern, just a few feet from the ground.

More mysterious is the sudden and peculiar failure of car engines a few yards further along on the Canterbury Road East, where the map suggests another road existed leading from Little Cliffsend to Ozengell Grange. Brakes have suddenly failed to respond and, according to Ted Harrison of the *Kent Messenger*, vehicles have veered away uncontrollably to cause horrifying accidents. Reliable witnesses have confirmed the sight of cars and vans rapidly moving away from their obvious route, for no apparent reason. The first fatal crash here occurred in 1922, since when there have been a large number of incidents. A spokesman said the police remain puzzled about the cause.

RECULVER
Reculver Towers

SOME five miles to the east of Herne Bay are the remains of St Mary's Church, but better known are the twin towers of Reculver at the original mouth of what was the River Wantsum, standing in the solitary landscape outlasting time and tide. The Roman fort of Regulbium, according to Caroline Hillier in her book *The Bulwark Shore*, was probably the only specifically military post south of the Humber and east of the Severn, after the initial Roman landings. Most of the walls have been destroyed by the encroaching sea, but Trinity House was able to restore the Towers as a valuable landmark for shipping.

In September 1966, summer excavations inside the fort revealed a substantial Roman building, with brick and masonry walls partly uncovered and inside, ten domestic ovens, implying its use as a bakehouse. What astounded the archaeologists though, was that when two cuts were made through part of the walls they revealed the skeltons of two babies; a third was then found in the corner. All three were of children less than six months old when they were buried, presumably in some pagan ritual which are often termed as 'foundation deposits'.

What, if any, these discoveries had to do with the most recent paranormal report, is not known, but during the summer of 1996, police were called to investigate the sightings of two hooded figures moving around in the vicinity of the Towers. They had been witnessed on more than one occasion by different witnesses over several months, but always in the early evening. When greeted, both forms faded away.

Allied to this, reports of the sound of a crying child were received up to quite recent times.

ROCHESTER

Guildhall

IN the early 1960s divers searching a wreck near the Scilly Isles discovered a solid silver plate, engraved with the heraldic arms of Sir Cloudesley Shovell – thus supplying proof that the remains of the vessel were those of his flagship *Association*, which sank in 1707.

Sir Cloudesley, born in Norfolk, became MP for Rochester in 1698. Among reminders of his visits to the town are the Corn Exchange, which he had built in 1706, the ornate plaster ceiling in the Guildhall, and the town clock. After his ship and three others wwere wrecked on the rocks during a tremendous storm, the Admiral's body was eventually washed up on the beach at Port Hellick and returned to London for a suitable ceremonial funeral.

Over the years his ghost, wearing full naval uniform, was seen many times, walking through the passages and into some of the rooms of the Guildhall. But since the finding of his ship, his presence is now reported only as 'invisible hands opening doors' or simply 'feeling his presence push past you'. What could be seen as an interesting aspect of the sinking of the *Association* is that it was blamed, by some, on a curse of a sailor who had been unjustly condemned to death by the Admiral.

ST MARY CRAY

White Swan

The pub dates from about 1850, but could be linked to a much older building in the locality. The haunting here is of the 'normal' poltergeist variety, with glasses .falling off a shelf and on one occasion a pewter mug unaccountably hitting owner Norman Pointer on the back, but with the added interest of an arparition named 'Jack'.

'No one seems worried by him,' Norman said. 'He was clearly seen walking through the bottom bar quite recently by one of my relatives, and by a number of customers earlier in the year. We have heard that an elderly man hanged himself in the cellars in the early 1900s. Perhaps this is connected.'

The unknown man was deseribed as being rather gloomy in appearance; as with others, no sooner is he noticed, than he disappears.

SANDGATE

Royal Norfolk Hotel

AN unknown urchin boy haunts this hotel in the pleasant seaside suburb of Folkestone.

Several members of the staff have seen the little fellow and been able to provide excellent detail of his appearance, without so far gaining any identification or discovering the cause for his visitations. He is always seen on the stairs, often silently crying his eyes out, but when approached by a sympathetic witness, he just disappears. He is described as being about nine years old, with blue eyes and wearing brown ragged clothing, 'a sort of Charles Dickens' character'. Also associated with his arrival, are the noises of moving furniture echoing from an empty room, the whoosh of a swinging rope and the unaccountable slamming of doors.

Those sensitive visitors who have so far failed to notice the young lad, have nevertheless admitted to feeling extremely sad at a certain spot on the stairs, whilst others claim that they feel the presence of a young entity that needs comforting.

Ship Inn

ONE night a few years ago, shortly after this traditional pub in the High Street had emptied of most of its customers, Stewart Whiffen, the landlord, was chatting with a friend, when suddenly he realised that his companion was transfixed, with his hair on end, staring at the end of the bar counter. He had just seen a woman in Victorian clothing, wearing a bonnet, all grey in colour, vanish as he watched, 'He was mystified and a bit perturbed, Stewart said. But this was not the only occasion that the woman had been observed in recent times, for only days earlier, the same figure had been seen to walk

Ship Inn, Sandgate

down the passageway between the front and rear bars, before fading into nothingness .

Of interest to the technically minded is that a more recent incident was the woman's appearance on the TV security monitor. One of the staff went into the corridor to investigate and was seen on the screen by his colleague to walk straight through the figure of an unknown female. The young man allegedly felt and saw nothing unusual, whilst the shape of the Victorian phantom just slowly dispersed, leaving only the rough outline of the face, until that too faded away. It is a great pity that no video recording equipment was available at the time.

More recently a woman customer saw the figure in the lavatories.

SEVENOAKS

Blighs Hotel

In mediaeval times Blighs was a farm, thought to be the home farm of the Archbishop of Canterbury's holding, It is believed that in Tudor times the property was called 'The Farm on The Vine' (the area once termed Sevenoaks Vine formed a large acreage to the north). In May 1646 the parish church of St Botolph Without at Bishopsgate purchased from John Turner 'a capital messuage and a total of 74fi acres'. The messuage was not named but later generations have known it as Bethlehem Farm and, later, Blighs Farm.

It has been claimed, incorrectly, that this Kent farmhouse, or rather its grounds, were used as a sort of convalescent area for patients. To the south of the present day hotel, on old Botolph property, was Bligh's Brewery, still in active operation in Edwardian days.

In 1998 I spoke to Tracy King, the manageress, who had been in residence for only for a couple of months. She said that one of the ghosts she saw was identified by a psychic friend as either Arthur or Albert. He was between aged between fifty and sixty, wore dark clothing and had startling ginger hair.

There was a young girl with him, also with ginger hair, and Tracy described her as having a weathered look. She appeared to be about fourteen or fifteen.

Tracy saw the couple when preparing for customers on her first Sunday morning in the hotel, at about midday. She glanced towards the bar, and was astonished to see the man leaning on the bar. He was wearing what looked like a black cardigan and a white shirt. The couple just faded away before Tracy could see much of the girl. Rumour has it that 'Arthur' in the 1960s, or perhaps a little earlier, was the owner or landlord. He became an alcoholic and either hanged himself, or was hanged for some terrible crime. A number of friends and customers have seen both of the former occupants of the hotel.

Emily Jackson House

IN the early Victorian era, tuberculosis was still a horrifying disease affecting large numbers of the population, but more noticeably the younger generation, and it was during this period that a young Sevenoaks woman, Emily Jackson, who was married to an architect, became deeply concerned at the lack of facilities for sufferers in the town. She adopted a baby with tuberculosis, and this created such an interest and support from among her friends that she decided, with her husband, to build a special home to treat children suffering from the disease. Her husband was later knighted for his work in designing the building and, with his wife, in setting up the charity.

The Emily Jackson Home became well known as a local charitable hospital for children with tuberculosis and poliomyelitis. The Jacksons lived on the ground floor of the building, leaving the top storey as a store-room and accomodation for staff. Emily continued to supervise the administration of the home until she died in 1902. During the First World War the building was used as a convalescent home for troops, but later reverted to being a home for infected children.

In 1984 a threat was made to close the unit, by then closely associated with Sevenoaks Hospital, but the protest campaign arranged by Rita Hargreaves, the sister in charge, ensured that the home and its facilities would remain, catering for adults as well as youngsters, although under a different system.

During the Christmas of 1984, a nursing auxiliary living in the top floor reported to Mrs Hargreaves that one of the patients, a woman, went into her room the previous evening and sat in the armchair looking out of the window. She asked her to go back downstairs, but was ignored, so tried to get the woman's attention by throwing a teddy bear at her. Allegedly it went right through her and she vanished. The nurse said that the visitor was wearing 'a sort of greyish uniform with epaulettes on her shoulders'. The description

71

matched that of Emily Jackson in an early nursing uniform.

Since then the home has been sold to a.new nursing organisation but reports continue to be made about a woman in a uniform sitting in a window on the top floor.

Ightham Mote

D ESCRIBED as the most complete small manor house in England, 14th century Ightham Mote takes its name from the Norman French word for the moat that surrounds the property.

One of the first owners was Sir Thomas Cawne who lived there for more than thirty years, until his death in 1374. The manor was then taken over by the Haut family, one of whom accompanied Edward V on his journey to London in 1483 with the intention of seizing the throne, following the death of Edward IV.

In 1957 Charles Robinson bought the property and, after carrying out extensive restoration, bequeathed the manor to The National Trust.When, in the 1970s, I asked him about the possibility of his home being haunted, he replied: 'Only by happy souls, no ghosts'.

However, I was told in 1997 by Bernadette Gillow of The National Trust that the previous owner, Sir Thomas Colyer-Fergusson, had organised a 'mass with intent' in the house and Charles Robinson had, at some time, followed this by arranging for an exorcism, although why is not known.

In 1872 a blocked cupboard door in an area adjoining the Great Hall, was opened to reveal the skeleton of a seated female. No details of her age or the reason for the entombment were ever established.

In 1993 Pam Chandler of Battle visited Ightham with a friend and was suddenly and inexplicably affected by a bout of severe shivering when at the top of the stairs near the Tudor Chapel. The following year, I was told by another visitor that she had been so badly affected by similar symptoms that a custodian had suggested an early visit to the doctor, after an emergency nurse had provided treatment.

Old guide books used to mention, but no longer do so, that a young girl had been stabbed in the vicinity many years ago, and occasionally staff hear that a visitor has seen the wraith of a girl.

Knole Park

A COTTAGE in the grounds of this 15th century manor house was affected by an unknown entity when it was occupied in 1974 by one of the war dens and his family. On returning from the garden one afternoon, the tenant's wife went to check on her young son, and was shocked to see the figure of a stranger approaching the bedroom containing the child. She rushed towards him, demanding to know who he was, and what he was doing in her home, but he vanished when she was only about ten feet away. Her husband later admitted seeing a vague outline in the upstairs corridor on occasions, but had been reluctant to mention the incidents, for fear of scaring his family.

Whether this building is the one that Vita Sackville-West felt unhappy about and which is supposed to contain 'a sinister atmosphere' sensed by occasional visitors, is not known. A young man who acted sometimes as altar boy in Knole Chapel, and at private evensong for Lord Sackville, claims to have seen the 'ghostly duchess' in the hornbeam avenue known as the Duchess Walk. It was thought to be the favourite area for the Duchess or Countess of Dorset, but is now believed to be the walk used by the victim of an unhappy Sackville marriage.

One of the large houses now incorporated into the Sevenoaks School complex is possibly also affected by the same phantom. A figure, wearing a dress of the 1770-1790 period, was seen crossing the road from Knole, a few feet above the road level. Her existence was accepted by members of the staff for many years, but there have been no recent reports of her.

SISSINGHURST

Castle Gardens

S ISSINGHURST Castle, in reality never more than a beautiful Elizabethan mansion built by the 'disreputable' Baker family of Cranbrook, was taken over for use as a prison for scores of soldiers captured during the Seven Year War with France shortly after Elizabeth ascended the throne.

In 1930 Sir Harold Nicolson and Vita Sackville-West bought what was by then a rather dilapidated ruin, and created the world famous gardens by which they, with their poems and books, are remembered.

As so frequently happens, stories arose about the castle and its ghosts, adding a thrilling and rather romantic aura to the estate. One tale relates that a priest was sealed up somewhere within the walls because of some terrible misdemeanour, and reports of hauntings continue to be reported.

Iris Hayter, one time housekeeper to Sir Harold, saw the figure of a tall thin man in a dark cloak walking towards the entrance, early one evening. When she called out, telling the visitor that the grounds and the castle were closed, the figure vanished in front of her. This was not the only occasion that the priest had been noticed, for several visitors have commented on the 'tall and striking figure of a cleric', walking near the Priest's House.

SMARDEN

Bakers Bridge

A PARTICULAR patch of road known as Maltman's Hill between Smarden and Pluckley seems to affect cars, or their drivers, at night. Residents in a cottage near the awkward bend in the road at Bakers Bridge, have heard unusual and inexplicable sounds, and associate them with the haunting by a monk at Dering Farm. There are a number of ghosts linked with Pluckley, but none, as far as is known, that have been experienced for at least thirty years, and certainly none of a monk, even though there are a number of religious associations with the area.

Quite a few drivers confirm that on the stretch of road just past Biddenden Green, their vehicles have suddenly stalled, but when examined, no faults were found.

Chequers Inn

I WAS delighted to find in 1997 that the licencees mentioned by Joan Forman in her book *Haunted South* (1978) are still in residence and Frank Stevens was able to assure me that the events detailed were completely accurate and that the mysterious phenomena continues to be experienced. A member of the staff had told me earlier that he had watched the door of room number six, the 'ghost room', open by itself, whilst Frank reported that one of the most recent incidents was when six old dinner plates suddenly appeared in the kitchen as he was preparing a meal. 'I have simply no idea where they came from', he assured me, 'but they proved to be very useful additions and helped to cater for the crowd that came in that day.' Yet a couple of days later, when he had planned for extra party requirements, the apports were nowhere to be found. They had vanished.

The weird incidents have been attributed to the invisible phantom of a young French prisoner-of-war who had been lodged in the Chequers, a 15th century building, during the Napoleonic wars, and had, for some unknown reason, been murdered there.

Smarden is only about six miles from where French prisoners were housed in Sissinghurst Castle and this haunting could well account for other paranormal incidents. On some mornings, having made up the beds after the departure of over-night guests, staff have often been puzzled by indentations on the covers, matching the human form. Normally this problem affects only room number six.

Windows originally shut have been found open, cutlery, like the plates, appears and then vanishes, an Afghan hound suddenly went berserk, an evening dress hung on top of a wardrobe

The Chequers, Smarden

was found to have travelled to the farthest end of the room.

Two sisters and their husbands who were staying in the pub for a weekend, in September 1997, had an unusual experience. One of the women woke to see the door of the bedroom open by itself to reveal the figure of a small, dark man standing there. When she called out he faded away. On the following night her sister was woken by something scratching her back, and her husband found the mark of an inverted cross on her skin. The following morning all four guests decided to leave rather abruptly.

TENTERDEN

Silver Hill

LATE one night in February 1997 Christine Hall, a teacher and lecturer from Cranbrook, was travelling home along the Ashford Road, after giving a talk to a local women's group and was approaching Silver Hill, when she noticed a young man in his early twenties, dressed in black rock and roll style with very tight trousers and a short jacket starting to cross the road just in front of her car. What stunned Christine was that she could see through the man as if he were made of semi-transparent plastic. So astounded was she that she failed to stop in time and was convinced that she had hit him. She turned round, expecting to see the figure lying on the road, but seeing it was clear, got out to search for signs of the accident. There were none. No dents. No scratches. Nothing. She returned home more than a little upset and 'utterly mystified'.

When tutoring an evening class at the school on Silver Hill for the WEA some years ago, I heard of a number of witnesses who had a similar experience in the same locality. It is encouraging to learn of an experience that confirms, it seems, the belief of a fatal accident in the area 'well within living memory', but any specific details would, I know, be welcomed.

TONBRIDGE
Cardinal's Error

O NE of the Kent pubs that is genuinely haunted, is this 17th century tavern on the outskirts of the town. It has long been associated with the phantom of a mysterious woman in a big hat who would enter one of the bedrooms, walk to the window and, apparently, throw herself out.

Valerie Green, wife of the owner Graham Green, had lived in the pub when she was a child, and she told me about a friendly woman she recalled, 'with a motherly appearance'. Over the years a number of visitors have reported seeing the apparent re-enactment of what seems to be a suicide, and also hearing the footsteps of the phantom in the corridor outside. Some small objects, such as a toby jug, and a pottery vase, have also been moved inexplicably.

Graham has been told that his unknown guest is in some way associated with a legendary tunnel that leads from the pub to the site of Summerhill Chapel, a couple of miles to the south east. There is another rumour that claims the woman is a victim of a drowning, which makes her appearance even more puzzling,

TUNBRIDGE WELLS
Binns Coffee Shop

ONE of the popular meeting places in the town is the Georgian arena of The Pantiles, and more especially perhaps, this teashop, where Beau Nash once held his social gatherings. But it is not this leader of fashion who frequents the premises.

An unidentified woman dressed in a long grey gown watches from a window on the first floor. Her face has never been seen, other than as a half silhouette

Cardinal's Error, Tonbridge

or in profile, and some witnesses, for there are many, believe that she may be Sarah Porter, an assistant to the fashion king whose duties were to watch out for newcomers to The Pantiles and to ensure that their subscriptions – to a club run by Beau Nash to maintain The Pantiles and, no doubt, himself – were collected.

Another more romantic suggestion is that she is a deserted bride, waiting for her bridegroom to arrive, and a third is that she may just be a former owner of the house, reluctant to leave what was her home. The current owner, John Bath, one of the scores of witnesses, thinks that the shade is that of a Madam who is waiting for one of her girls to return to what was her house of ill repute.

Tiles Restaurant

HERE is another eating house that is home to an unknown spectre. A few years ago, when the Chalet Arosa Restaurant occupied the premises, Pat Humphreys, the manager, had an experience he will never forget. He was asleep in one of the staff bedrooms, and was woken by the sudden intense drop in temperature and the appearance of a weird light on the wall. The glow slowly took shape until it materialised into the figure of a carpenter, complete with apron, who moved across the room, and disappeared through the opposite wall.

Although the Chowdhurrys, who own the restaurant now, have never noticed anything unusual, they do suffer a few poltergeist incidents in their kitchen and on the stairs. 'Things move around and we hear the sound of plates crashing, and sometimes an occasional footstep, but we have never found anything to explain these funny noises,' Mr Chowdhurry said.

The Gem Shop

GEOFFREY Butler, owner of this specialist shop in The Pantiles, told me of an unusual incident experienced by a carpenter carrying out the restoration of the cellar some twenty years ago.

The chippy had been warned by the electrician, who was up-dating the power supply system in the same area, that he was about to turnoff the mains, but unbeknown to the carpenter, he moved upstairs to check the wiring on another floor.

The carpenter carried on with his work whilst chatting to his invisible colleaue, whom he sensed was still only a couple of feet away. But when he turned round, having received no response to some comment, discovered that he was alone. The noises of somebody working continued, but there was nothing to see. Geoffrey feels that the incident could be associated with a ghostly figure he had noticed in the adjoining cellars on more than one occasion.

Mulberry Lake

THERE is a large pond known as the Mulberry Lake on Bishop's Down in the Rusthall Park area adjoining Denny Bottom, which once formed a part of a large estate of a huge mansion that was destroyed by fire years ago.

The only evidence of the existence of the property today is part of the outer wall surrounding the estate.

The trees, shrubs and thick undergrowth act as a barrier for anyone but keen walkers and anglers.

Local man Tony Tidey, with his colleague Kevin, thought that the lake might be worth trying for a few tench, so one evening, having parked their van at the roadside near an old well, proceeded to push through the thick brambles to the lake.

There were a few other optimists waiting for a bite, but shortly before the sun finally set, the couple realised that they were alone.

After a few minutes of waiting in silence, Tony heard the sound of running footsteps along the path skirting the edge of the lake, yet despite flashing his torch in the direction of the runner, could see nothing. The invisible visitor returned two or three times within a few minutes but there was never anything to see to account for the noise. Although Kevin was sitting a mere twenty five yards away he heard nothing, but admitted that he felt so uncomfortable and uneasy, as if being watched, that he decided to pack up for the night.

Some eighteen months later, the anglers learnt of a possible cause for the inexplicable sound. During the Civil War, a group of Cromwellians had deliberately set fire to the manor house and a number of servants trapped inside were burnt to death. Two or three, in trying to escape the murderers, ran towards the lake, but were either shot or were drowned.

Nobody fishes the Mulberry Lake any more.

Rusthall

THE Beacon in Tea Garden Lane has an unusual history, for when it was known as Rusthall Beacon, it was used as a sanctuary for six young Basque refugees from the Spanish Civil War. Then, in 1939, it provided a similar function for a group of Austrian Jewish girls who had escaped from Hitler's storm troopers.

In the post-war years Beacon House was a guest house until, in 1959, a Mr Dean bought the property to convert it to an hotel. Some thirty years later, Ellie Goodrich, the then owner, became aware of bottles and glasses being thrown about by an unseen force, and the sound of a telephone could be heard ringing in a couple of rooms where no such equipment existed.

Her chef also complained of the row made by youngsters running up and down the stairs, when there were no such guests staying at the hotel.

One afternoon Frank Goodrich and his wife were lunching with a guest, when their friend saw, from the corner of his eye, a mysterious figure knock over one of the glasses on the dresser.

Seconds later a full bottle leapt off the top of the shelf and landed, intact, on the floor.

Late in 1997 I spoke to the current owner, John Cullen, who had seen nothing out of the ordinary, but two young girls staying in the hotel had seen the vague shape of a man standing at the top of the stairs one afternoon, and asked who he was. 'I naturally had to say that I was unable to help, but they didn't seem worried about him, they were just curious, as I am.'

Upper Grosvenor Road

ENTHUSIASTIC chess player Deirdre Morris noticed, shortly after her husband David's death, that the chess pieces she had set up for the next game were being moved around, and she believes her late husband was responsible.

'I think David is here and trying to reassure me that I'll come to no harm,' she told me. Her husband was also very keen on growing roses and twice Deirdre has found freshly cut white roses either in a vase of which he was fond or sometimes next to her break-fast plate. David was also, it seems, a bit fussy about the downstairs curtains, always insisting that they be drawn together, but after the funeral and 'to show that things change, I would merely throw the curtains together in rather a slap-happy fashion and then go shopping, only to find, when I got back, that they had been brought tightly together as if to say, 'that's not right, I'll just straighten them up', Deirdre said.

Deirdre Morris with the chess set whose pieces have moved mysteriously

Deirdre finds glasses are tied up with string and and ribbons are scattered around on the floor making unusual, but definite patterns.

'When I went into the kitchen the other day, for example,' she told me, 'there, on the floor, made with some coloured tape, were a couple of anniversary dates, one being of the sixth of August – a day of great significance to me'.

Desk top objects moved to form the shape of a cross

WALMER

Saxon Shore Way

ALTHOUGH Middle Street in Deal contains, it is claimed, no less than nine haunted houses, the reports up to a few years related mainly to unidentified property or houses that were suffering from some form of poltergeist trouble, which normally ceases within a few months of being reported, or even embellished legends without much substance. One of these, I think, is that of the Wandering Piper who, unseen, plays his bagpipes around the streets in the evenings, but of course 1 could be wrong.

Walmer Castle, to the south, despite its historical associations, has no ghosts, or hauntings, but on the Saxon Shore Way, there have been a number of reports of a woman in Victorian clothing seen during the early evenings, striding along the coastal path to Kingsdown about a mile away. One cannot but help wonder if she is in any way associated with Lady Hester Stanhope, the eccentric virago who termed herself 'Queen of the Arabs'. It was she who cared for William Pitt the Younger during his last days, and later arranged for most of the gardens at Walmer Castle to be constructed.Or is she connected with the Duke of Wellington, perhaps, who died in the castle in 1852?

When greeted by anyone, the figure stops, turns and fades away.

WEST MALLING

West Malling Aerodrome

ONCE used as a back-up airfield for Biggin Hill during the Battle of Britain era, West Malling aerodrome exists only as a memory, with its control tower and a couple of huts as reminders for the area is now shared by a housing estate and a golf course. At the last air show to be held there, in 1982, one of the young assistants helping with the event, commented on 'the handsome young pilot in his flying gear, and his glorious old black and white dog', seen walking around the show. But it seems that there were only a few of her colleagues who saw the figures. There was no record of such a visitor or staff member, but some of the former RAF visitors, on being questioned, recalled one of their group who fitted the description.

Also associated with that period, but in the 1950s, was the wraith of a air man in flying uniform, seen on a number of occasions peering through a window of the council offices, formerly the officers' mess, and the sighting of a solitary pilot walking past what was once the guard room.

Confirmation of the haunting was provided when a television company was filming sequences for *We'll Meet Again* in the 1980s, and the director asked that two airmen and a WAAF be moved out of camera shot. They were apparently examining the engine of a jeep, a vital prop in one of the scenes, but when approached by an assistant cameraman, the group of three vanished in front of him.

The Bakery Lounge

The Bakery Lounge

THE Bakery Lounge, now a restaurant, was originally a mediaeval hall house of about 1450 on the site of some abbey buildings. The house offered accommodation for monks and visiting dignitaries whilst the cellars provided prison facilities for the criminal element of the town. This jail was in use right up to the 1700s. One of the building's upper rooms houses a figure wearing the dark habit of a monk, who has been seen sitting crouched over an ancient desk, writing. After a few seconds he gently drifts away. He was last observed in 1985, and was occasionally joined by an unseen presence which has been felt in the room which immediately backs on to the study. So far no-one has so far been able to identify either of the entities.

The Bear Inn

ONE of the many old buildings of the High Street, the Bear Inn, built about 1685, was once the home of a Captain Lucas. When he married, he moved away from the town, although still returns to the tavern, to walk along a corridor leading to his former bedroom.

The son of a former owner of the inn, whose bedroom was that used by the Captain, would often notice the figure of a naval officer standing in the corner of the room, and chat to him before going to sleep, thinking that he was just a

82

friend of his father.

It was only some years later when he and his parents moved to another pub, and he related his experiences to them, did the lad realise that he had been conversing with a spectre, or so the story goes. It seems more likely that the apparition had been witnessed perhaps a couple of times just before the boy had fallen asleep, and affected and formed part of a vivid dream.

Nevertheless, quite recently the Captain has been seen and reported by several independent witnesses, walking the same corridor.

Foxed and Bound Bookshop

The Bear Inn

MARGARET Gadd in her book about hauntings in the town, records that she witnessed the ghost that resides in this ancient building, which was once a barn for the Malt House that forms the Colonnade.

The frequently seen phantom is that of an unknown woman who appears from the fireplace area on the ground floor, to wander across what was originally the living room. This was probably part of the next door building when

it consisted of a single property, for the shape disappears on reaching a cupboard hiding a bricked up doorway leading to the adjoining house.

Added to this haunting, is that of a man who rushes up stairs which were actually removed following a renovation project some years ago. It is this revenant that Margaret witnessed when moving her carpet. 'My impression,' she says, 'was that of a thickset man in his forties, who was wearing a caped coat, similar to that of the Victorian times. He just bundled me out of the way as he rushed past.'

It was in the 1940s that two sisters, who were then living there, noticed

Foxed and Bound

83

the sound of someone dragging himself up the stairs, groaning and panting as if badly hurt, or carrying a very heavy object. The noise would immediately stop when another member of the family arrived and called out a greeting.

Another peculiarity is the sound of an invisible somebody playing a tune on crockery in the larder. It is likely that the unseen visitor may have been a victim of the fighting during the Civil War, Margaret believes, for the town was host to a number of Cromwellian soldiers waiting the arrival of Colonel Fairfax, before the Battle of Maidstone a few miles away.

Douce's Manor

BETWEEN the parish church of St Mary the Virgin and St Leonard's Tower is this intriguing manor, which is much older than its 18th century appearance. It is haunted by a fair-haired woman dressed in Edwardian clothing, who was first reported when the house was converted to an hotel.

Local author, Margaret Gadd, tells of two young men who had been sleeping in one of the attic rooms; one woke suddenly to see his companion shouting and writhing about. Apparently 'the Edwardian lady' had shaken him awake to ask him a question that he was unable to understand. This could well have been part of a dream, but a former employee of the owners also admitted seeing the ghost and received 'a sort of an answer' when, thinking that she was a visitor in fancy dress, he had asked her if he could assist in any way. The identifying name he received in response was 'The Merry Widow of Mereworth', who was actually a resident of the manor in 1850.

When the building was requisitioned as a billet for RAF personnel during the Second World War the cellar was used as a recreation room and many of the pilots left their signatures on the ceiling as reminders of their stay. One of them still makes an occasional 'return visit', having been observed on more than one occasion walking round one end of the room.

WOOTTON

The Endeavour

JUST above Denton, at the junction of Wootton Hill, is this ancient pub, which is haunted by a monk. Ian Cook, the current landlord, was originally highly sceptical, even though the previous tenant, Stephen Taylor had often heard the sound of footsteps in the empty room above the bar. Stephen had also reported the figure of monk wearing a brown habit, sitting at a table near the fireplace, whilst a number of regular customers confirmed that they too had witnessed the unknown apparition, although a couple had noticed him walk the same route as the footsteps when upstairs.

It is believed that some 200 years ago a priest named Matthew was found guilty of raping the daughter of a local landlord and was hanged for the crime. His body was displayed in a gibbet for a short time, only to be removed and later discovered in the garden of the Endeavour. Finally the corpse was put into the cellar of the pub, a part of which was then bricked up. It is said that barrels stored near that part of the wall are often found to have been moved, and beer taps have been turned off.

SELECT BIBLIOGRAPHY

Bulwark Shore, Caroline Hillier, Granada, 1982
Curious Kent, John E Vigar, Meresborough Books, 1984
Discovering Kent, Marcus Crouch, Shire Publications, 1975
Ghost Stories from Faversham, Griselda Cann, Winterwood Books, 1995
Ghosts of Today, Andrew Green, Kaye & Ward, 1980
Ghosts of West Malling, Margaret Gadd, privately published, 1997
Haunted Churches of England, Graham J McEwan, Robert Hale, 1989
Haunted Houses, Andrew Green, Shire Publications, 1996
*Haunted Inns & Tavern*s, Andrew Green, Shire Publications, 1995
Haunted Lives, Peter Mullen, Robert Hale, 1996
Haunted Pub Guide, Guy Lyon Playfair, Harrap,1985
Haunted Shepway, Paul Harris, private published, 1995
Haunted South, Joan Forman, Robert Hale, 1978
Kent Village Book, Alan Bignell, Countryside Books, 1986
Pantiles Ghosts, Geoffrey Butler, private published, 1996
Pleasant Town of Sevenoaks, Sir John Dunlop, Caxton & Holmesdale, 1964
Theatre Ghosts, Roy Harley Lewis,David & Charles, 1988
Tonbridge Tales, John Hilton, privately published, 1980(?)
Unexplained Kent, ed Brian Paine with Trevor Sturgess, Breedon Books, 1997
Weekend Haunts, Robin Mead, Impact Books, 1994

Newspapers and journals

Evening Standard
Faversham Times
Guide to English Heritage Properties (1992 edition)
Gulf News
Images of War (No 3) (Marshall Cavendish)
Kent Life (November 1978)
Kent Messenger
Kent Today (December 1996)
The National Trust Handbook (1996 edition)
Nursing Times (Volume 86, number 50, 1990)

About the author

The author, para-psychologist Andrew Green, pictured at Dreamland Fun Park, Margate (see page 54), when he appeared on the ITV Strange But True series in November 1997.

Andrew Green, BSc, MPhil, FETC, has been a member of the Society for Psychical Research since 1972, has written a number of books and articles on ghosts and hauntings, edited three recent works on specific phenomena and appeared in numerous radio and television programmes.

In 1966 he was commissioned to investigate alleged phenomena in the Royal Albert Hall and later in the Dreamland Fun Park at Margate, both being featured in television programmes.

PICTURE CREDITS